The

Raw

Transformation

The *Raw* Transformation

Energizing Your Life with Living Foods

WENDY RUDELL

Foreword by David Wolfe

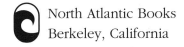
North Atlantic Books
Berkeley, California

Published by
North Atlantic Books
P.O. Box 12327
Berkeley, California 94712

Photographs by Geno Perches, except photo on page 27 by Bruce Herman and photos on 34, 88, and 148
Cover design by Suzanne Albertson
Book design by Francisco Rincón and Paula Morrison

Printed in the United States of America

The Raw Transformation: Energizing Your Life with Living Foods is sponsored by the Society for the Study of Native Arts and Sciences, a nonprofit educational corporation whose goals are to develop an educational and crosscultural perspective linking various scientific, social, and artistic fields; to nurture a holistic view of arts, sciences, humanities, and healing; and to publish and distribute literature on the relationship of mind, body, and nature.

North Atlantic Books' publications are available through most bookstores. For further information, call 800-337-2665 or visit our website at www.northatlanticbooks.com.

Substantial discounts on bulk quantities are available to corporations, professional associations, and other organizations. For details and discount information, contact our special sales department.

Library of Congress Cataloging-in-Publication Data
Rudell, Wendy.
    The raw transformation : energizing your life with living foods / Wendy
Rudell ; foreword by David Wolfe.
        p. cm.
    Includes bibliographical references and index.
    ISBN-13: 978-1-55643-589-8 (pbk.)
    ISBN-10: 1-55643-589-4 (pbk.)
    1. Cookery (Natural foods) 2. Raw foods. I. Title.
    TX741.R82 2006
    641.5'63--dc22
                                                            2006018691

2 3 4 5 6 7 8 9 UNITED 12 11 10 09 08 07

Table of Contents

Part 1: Introduction to the Raw Lifestyle

Part 2: Food Preparation Basics

Part 3: Recipes for Health and Beauty

Part 4: Final Tidbits

Foreword

I first met Wendy while she was working at the Optimum Health Institute in San Diego, California. Back then, I used to sneak into the center to give secret lectures about raw food in the back room, and later Wendy and I would spend hours in the kitchen concocting all kinds of outrageous dishes. She has always had the most creative and delicious ways of presenting raw cuisine—she puts a lot of love into everything she does, and it shows.

Needless to say, I no longer have to sneak into retreat centers to speak about raw food, and similarly, Wendy has taken her knowledge of food and health to the next level. When she told me that she was working on a raw recipe book, I knew right away that it was going to be the best book on living cuisine ever. Wendy's knowledge of health and nutrition is world class—she is the very best at what she does, and this book is a clear reflection of that expertise. I sincerely doubt if anyone on Earth is more qualified to create a book like this. With thirty years of experience in the field, she is truly in a category all her own.

Wendy speaks across the generational gap as well. She comes from an older community of healers, deeply involved in the teachings of Ann Wigmore and the wisdom of sprouted foods and wheatgrass juice. But Wendy's energy, open-mindedness, and focus on nutrient-dense super-foods speak directly to the younger generation of people eager to learn about the newest health technologies. What results is a perfect fusion of the tried-and-true with the up-and-coming. Raw food isn't what it used to be, after all. At one point in time, all a health seeker had to choose from was conventional grocery store produce and wheatgrass. While those things are inarguably great, we now know there is a whole world of raw organic super-foods available to us, and it would be silly not to give ourselves every advantage we possibly can. That is why the recipes in this book are so special. They have been crafted with much more than just flavor in mind; Wendy has found a way to work that extra nutritional edge into each bite.

The Raw Transformation is by far the best book of its kind. I am so thankful that Wendy has taken the time to put all of her great ideas on paper, to share them with the world. This book is more in line with my personal philosophies on nutrition and living food than any recipe book before it. Wendy has taken the most delicious, nutritious food in the world and synergized it into individual living masterpieces of raw and living food cuisine. I believe that anyone can benefit tremendously from including Wendy's delicious recipes in their diet, whether you've been a raw-food enthusiast for thirty years or never even heard of wheatgrass. This book makes the sunfood diet (a raw plant-food diet) appealing to even the most discriminating of palates.

So take in Wendy's experience, cuisine, love, and HAVE THE BEST DAY EVER!

—Dr. David Wolfe
    San Diego, California
    May 2006

Acknowledgments

I want to first thank all of the guests of the Optimum Health Institute for their encouragement and support in getting me to promise to write a gourmet raw recipe book. Working with them was such an inspiration and gave me the confidence to make this dream a reality.

Thanks also to my dear friend David Wolfe for his constant support over the years and for his knowledge and the many books that were an inspiration to me in embracing this lifestyle. He continues to be my mentor and raw-food guru.

Sara from Rawfood.com reviewed this book and gave many valuable suggestions to make this the best raw-cuisine book ever. She also turned me onto maca, cacao, coconut butter, goji berries, and so many other high-energy, high-antioxidant foods. (See Resources list.)

I extend my deep appreciation to Geno, my photographer, who patiently displayed the dishes in ways to bring out the best in them, using a more natural lighting and setting that fits the Raw concept.

Francisco Rincón, Oscar, and Rosie provided creative contributions to the layout and design. They did a great job in making this book flow nicely with the text and photos.

I want to thank all of my friends who tasted my recipes over the years and gave me the honest feedback as to which ones I should include in this edition. You all know who you are.

A special thanks to Erwin Verburgt from www.casabeard.com in Cabo San Lucas, Mexico, for allowing us to display our recipes on his beautiful dishware. Erwin, the photos would not have been the same without your support. Thank you.

A special thanks also goes to Jacobo Turquie, from La Panga Restaurant in San Jose Del Cabo, whose assistance and support in the presentation of our dishes was so much appreciated. For the best food ever in Southern Baja, check out www.lapanga.com.

ix

I thank my parents and close family who were always encouraging me to complete this book despite the many challenges I had to overcome.

Last but not least I want to thank my partner Charles Free. If not for him, this book would have remained a dream in my mind. He was a persistent push in getting me started, which is half the battle in writing a manuscript. Thank you, my dear, for all your suggestions and support and for believing in me. I love you.

—Wendy Rudell
Cabo San Lucas, Mexico
2006

Introduction

Although this book is primarily a gourmet raw-food recipe book, I have included information about how transformation can happen for us through not only diet but yoga, breath work, meditation, and bio-energetic resonance, bringing us more joy, abundance, and optimum health.

My childhood was an interesting one, to say the least. I was born just outside Toronto, Canada, to parents who were very adventurous and somewhat untraditional. When I was a year and a half old, my parents decided to pack up the family and move to Trinidad, a small island in the West Indies just off the coast of Venezuela.

The first ten years of my life I lived on this tropical island with all that that lifestyle has to offer. I was addicted to the ocean, to the sun, to climbing coconut trees, foraging for wild tropical fruits, and playing hide-and-go-seek with the jungle monkeys. I grew up in this environment that was quite wild and free. I think the Raw Living Foods Lifestyle resonates most with my childhood, and perhaps this is why it comes so naturally to me.

I returned to Canada to complete my education and for years felt like a fish out of water. Living in a cold climate, bundled up most of the year, and far away from the ocean made me feel very repressed. Something was missing. It wasn't until I took a vacation to Hawaii that I realized what that was.

I left Canada shortly after that, making Hawaii my new home. Slowly my vitality and enthusiasm for life were reborn. The warm weather, the ocean, fresh air, and the abundance of fresh raw fruits and vegetables rejuvenated my body and soul. I felt there was a message in living a simple natural lifestyle in a warm nurturing environment. I wanted to learn more and share this information with the millions of people who are stuck in the cities, caught up in the traffic of life, and plagued with every disease in the book.

Learning about nutrition and natural living became my mission. I studied yoga, massage, nutrition, colon cleansing, breath work, and anything else that would assist my journey and help me move towards optimum health and well-being. It became very clear to me that the mind, body, and spirit are interconnected, and food (diet) is an important piece in all that.

I came to realize that eating raw foods has a biochemical effect on the brain and a direct effect on the mind/body connection. All foods have a vibratory frequency and a direct response in the body (as everything is interconnected). The body has memory and is evolving. Eating a ripe organic papaya full of enzymes and nutrients has a much different response in the body than a piece of barbequed meat. I intuited that raw living foods could be an evolutionary tool and an important key in raising our vibrational frequency.

My conviction grew during my five-year employment at the Optimum Health Institute in San Diego, California. I saw amazing transformation happen in peoples' lives on all levels. The Optimum Health Institute (OHI) is a cleansing and detoxification retreat center where people can go to cleanse their bodies and learn about the mind-body connection. Here I taught classes in yoga, breath work, nutrition, gourmet raw-food preparation, and how to live a more "raw," natural lifestyle. It was here that I started to develop the concept "Transform 2000," a healing process designed to raise the consciousness of the planet. This would include the modalities of yoga, breath work, raw living foods, fasting, bio-energetic medicine (QXCI/SCI0),* meditation, and anything else that would transform our lives, bring us more connection with our Higher Self, and provide a greater sense of health and well-being.

I am presently living and continuing to work with these modalities just outside Cabo San Lucas, Mexico. Here I teach classes in yoga, breath work, and raw foods and work with individuals or small groups as a health and nutritional lifestyle coach. In the following pages you will find basic theory about preparing raw cuisine, guidelines to making healthier choices, information on other transformational modalities, and some "awesome raw-some" recipes.

---

*Quantum Xeroid Consciousness Interface device/Scientific Consciousness Interface Operations device, the biofeedback device that I mention in these pages.

Part 1

Introduction to the Raw Lifestyle

Why Eat Raw?

Many of you may be asking yourself what that means—"Raw." You may think that eating a piece of fruit, a salad, ceviche, or sashimi would fall into that category, and how boring if that was all there were to it! The following recipes should offer you a most delightful perspective on what raw foods really can be. Nature's abundance is limitless, not only in the many textures, but in the variety of colors and tastes. I especially like to create meals that have rich contrasting colors and distinct, yet subtle, flavors.

The most nutritious of raw foods are the living raw foods. These are foods that are still growing, like sprouts and germinated nuts and seeds. The young green shoots from certain seeds, which offer so much taste and nutrition, also fall into this category. These foods are full of enzymes, plant hormones, oxygen, vitamins, and minerals. They have such a high vibrational charge to them that when viewed with Kirlian photography, the aura or energetic field of these foods indicates a life force that is non-existent (or dead) in cooked foods.

David Wolfe, the world's most renowned raw-food lecturer and author, gives us some incredible photos in his book *Eating for Beauty.* The life charge is visible around different fruits and vegetables. It is this life force that feeds our mind-body connection and helps to heal us. One day mainstream medicine will acknowledge the healing powers of foods, and we will turn to our gardens once more to bring our bodies back to balance and optimum health.

Ecologically, it makes so much more sense to eat raw living foods because we are not consuming processed goods or contributing to the accumulation of garbage on this planet by requiring a lot of packaging. All the wastes from my kitchen end up in the compost, so I'm actually giving back to the Earth.

Adopting a raw-food lifestyle does not support the killing and torturing of animals that are grown for consumption, nor does it contribute to deforestation for fuel. Two-thirds of the world's population lives in developing countries where they must burn wood or charcoal for cooking fuel. Not only is

this disturbing to the balance of nature globally, but this disturbance is reflected in the health of the bodies that continue to deny "Nature's First Law," which is "EAT RAW"!

According to David Wolfe, eighty percent of all species on this planet enjoy optimum health, and not one of them is cooking their food. Think of it—man is the only one. Another thing to consider is the fact that humans have only had fire and the ability to cook food for a small percentage of time that we have existed on Earth. What did people do before that?

We are also now finding out that the human digestive system is designed to eat the raw foods that nature provides and is very similar to that of the gorilla, which is mainly vegetarian and lives mostly on the leaves, fruits, nuts, and berries in the jungle. Eating cooked foods consisting of animal proteins, fats, starches, and sugars, etc., not only robs our body of vital nutrients and enzymes, but causes fermentation and all kinds of degenerative disease. It may take thirty to forty years for the degeneration to manifest, but eventually the major organs and systems of the body will break down.

What
Happens When We Cook Food?

Whenever we cook a natural whole raw food, we alter the chemical structure of that food. It loses or gains components, making it quite unrecognizable as a whole food. When this happens, the messages sent to the brain basically say that the body is not getting what it needs to survive, and that a mutation has entered the body, which then stimulates the immune system to work harder to attack these foreign particles. In essence, the body identifies cooked food as a toxin. Scientific research shows us that after eating a meal of cooked food we develop a condition called digestive leukocytosis, where the white blood cell count rises in an effort to attack what has entered the body. This eventually weakens the immune system.

I recommend eating a minimum of 60 percent raw, and anything above that is doing yourself a favor. Try some of these recipes and get a new lease on life. Slowly try to incorporate more and more raw foods into your diet and feel once again what it's like to have limitless energy and a clear and focused mind. Most of all, enjoy the rich delicious tastes and pleasure that a raw cuisine can bring.

Whenever
we cook a natural
whole raw food we alter
the chemical structure
of that food.

Enzymes

Awareness is growing about enzymes in our foods and how they contribute to our overall health. What is an enzyme? It's an electrically charged protein molecule necessary for every process in the body. There are three different kinds of enzymes: The food enzymes that occur naturally in our raw and living foods; digestive enzymes produced by the human body to help break down food; and metabolic enzymes that are responsible for every chemical process in our cells.

We will not find one enzyme in cooked food because they are destroyed when heated above 115 degrees. Research has found that we have a finite amount of these enzymes—an enzyme pool, so to speak—in our cells. Imagine your enzyme pool like a bank account with a set amount deposited there. If we keep withdrawing these enzymes because we eat enzyme-deficient foods, the body will use up its reserves. Pretty soon we are overdrawn and that means big trouble. Our digestive processes will rob enzymes from other systems in the body, wearing down the body and making us vulnerable to disease. However, when we introduce enzyme-rich foods we are making a deposit to our account, and that additional deposit will be reflected in the vitality of our body and mind. These enzyme-rich living foods can then assist the body to digest food, lessening the burden on the digestive tract and replenishing the metabolic enzymes as well (so they don't become depleted too, leaving us feeling tired and achy).

There are many books currently available about enzymes (see Recommended Reading in the back of the book) that I invite you to read, as it will only add to your resolve in making an important lifestyle change.

Nutrichemicals and Phytochemicals

These are relatively new terms to most people. They are the elements found in raw and living foods that the plants manufacture to ward off diseases or gain protection from the environment. They can be likened to a plant's immune system and are high in antioxidants. Antioxidants "mop up" free radicals in the body that cause the body to age and eventually break down.

Oxygen

Oxygen is essential to human survival. We find this element in the air that we breathe,

the water that we drink, and the foods that we eat. Raw, unprocessed, organic foods have the highest amount of oxygen in them. When our body is oxygen-rich we feel energized and our mind is clear. You can do an experiment to test this idea. Have a big organic salad with a raw dressing on it and see how you feel. There isn't that heavy tired feeling that you get after eating a pizza and soda, hamburger, or steak and fries. These latter foods are heavy in cooked fats and proteins that have much less available oxygen, and in turn have to rob the body's cells of oxygen in order to metabolize them.

The other really cool thing about oxygen and a raw-food diet is that when you grow your sprouts or veggies in your garden you are actually generating oxygen on the planet. I tell people to grow their young sunflower greens, buckwheat greens, and wheatgrass in their homes so the air quality indoors can be improved. This is ideal, especially if you're living in the city where air quality is poor.

Hormones

These are phytochemicals and nutrients that exist in plants to strengthen their immunity to diseases and external stresses. Phytoestrogens are one example found in abundance in soy products. They are known to be helpful in the balancing of female hormones during menopause. The growing tips of sprouts and young shoots contain growth hormones that are both rejuvenating and regenerating to the cells of our body. When we ingest these youth-providing hormones, we can see this reflected in the quality and vitality of our skin, hair, and cells, giving us that youthful healthy glow.

Vitamins and Minerals

These components are found in all foods and are especially abundant in raw and living foods. When we cook our foods, much of the water- and fat-soluble vitamins are destroyed, leaving very little true nutrition. The minerals are still present, but without the enzymes to transport them into the cells, they too, get lost, leaving the body in a demineralized state. Osteoporosis is a classic example of what happens when the body becomes deficient in minerals. The body will then draw the minerals from the bones. This condition will also happen as the body tries to balance the acidity from eating the Standard American Diet (SAD). It draws the alkaline minerals such as calcium from the bones to neutralize the acid condition. Raw, organic foods are the best source of vitamins and minerals because they add minerals to the body and help keep the acid/alkaline balance in check. We end up being mineral-rich rather than mineral-depleted.

Organically grown foods have not been altered genetically or chemically. They have not been fertilized, dyed, radiated, sprayed with pesticides or herbicides, or altered in any other way. These are foods that have been fertilized with compost and other natural soil fertilization methods. Organic foods are abundant in trace minerals and have far less sugar content than their commercially grown, highly hybridized counterparts. In my opinion they also taste so much better. From my experience, not only is there enhanced flavor, but my cravings are diminished after eating these nutrient-packed foods.

The biggest complaint heard is that organic fruits and vegetables are too expensive compared to commercially grown produce, and they often lack "curb appeal" (or a marketable exterior). It may be that organic foods are cheaper in the long run because you are adding health to your body rather than disease, which can add up in medical bills down the road. You also get a lot more nutrient value per dollar in your organic foods.

It is true that organic foods can sometimes be smaller in size than a pumped-up hybrid and perhaps not as pretty. Because they are not grown with heavy insect sprays and chemicals to increase their size they may have an inferior appearance, but the health benefits far outweigh this difference. If the costs are an issue for you, try growing a garden in your back yard, visiting a farmer's market in your area, or possibly organizing a co-op where others can participate and collectively buy quantity at cost. There are many options for reducing the cost of organic foods. All of your sprouts you can grow very easily by yourself, and these are the best of all the raw organic foods because they are still living when you eat them.

Commercially Grown and Genetically Modified Foods

Commercially grown foods are those grown with mass production and extensive storage and shipping in mind. They are highly hybridized for the sake of consistent, pleasing appearance and convenience. Chemical fertilizers and

sprays are applied in abundance to these foods. They have far fewer minerals in them. The sugar content, especially in the hybridized fruits and vegetables, can be double what you'll find in organic foods.

The most hybridized are seedless fruits such as grapes and watermelon. Beets, carrots, corn, and potatoes are all highly hybridized. Even bananas are now so highly hybridized that I rarely eat them. The small young wild bananas are wonderful, though—if you can find them. You'll notice that the seeds are still in these bananas. The small wild organic bananas also make the best sorbets (ice creams). See the section on desserts.

Genetically engineered or GE foods are sometimes called "Frankenstein foods." They are genetically altered for specific purposes, usually to make them more resistant to insects or more responsive to chemical fertilizers. Unlike traditional breeding, genetically engineered foods are new life forms that would not normally occur in nature. To create these new foods, scientists are splicing genes from bacteria, viruses, other plants, animals, even humans, into our staple crops such as corn, soybeans, canola oil and cotton. Some examples of this include the use of fish genes in tomatoes and strawberries, and jellyfish genes in potatoes. These plants become infertile and will not seed, so the farmer is forced to go back to the big agribusiness companies to buy new seeds. These foods have not been tested for their effects on humans, nor are they adequately monitored or regulated. They have the potential to out-compete many native species.

We do not know what the long-term result of tampering with the food supply will be, but we already see adverse effects in nature. See the website www.truefoodnow.org for more information.

I urge everyone to write his or her legislative representatives and demand that the consumer be given information about what has been genetically altered so we have a clear choice as to what we put into our bodies. Europe is far ahead of the U.S. in this respect, with many countries requiring labels on packaging to identify GE food.

The details are controversial in regard to what constitutes good food combining, so I will share with you what I learned at OHI and what works for me. Each person is different and will have to find that balance for him- or herself. The guidelines here are based on how the body breaks down different foods with respect to the transit times through the stomach. I invite you to consider other people's ideas on food combining and then to decide for yourself what feels right for you. If you have digestive problems then it is wise to follow the "Rules of the Stomach" (see below). The recipes in this book are not always written with optimum food combining in mind, so if your intention is to strictly follow the rules then make the necessary substitutions or deletions in the recipes to fulfill that purpose.

Why Proper Food Combining?

Proper food combining respects the natural limits of the body's enzyme stores and its requirements for digestion and metabolism. It promotes efficient digestion and absorption of nutrients, reduces toxicity, and maximizes the cleansing properties of raw and living foods. As a result, proper food combining frees up our energy and allows the mind-body connection to once again speak to us, letting us know what is optimal for us and what is not.

Food combining becomes extremely important if your intention is to cleanse the body. A cleanse is a dietary regime that assists the body to detoxify from the accumulation of wastes and toxins; it usually consists of at least 80 percent raw foods. The higher the raw food intake, the deeper will be the cleanse.

Once the body has cleansed itself of stagnant toxicity and the digestive system is working optimally, then it can handle some improperly combined foods once in a while. Many people in the Raw Food Movement believe that if you are eating all raw, then food combining becomes irrelevant. I have heard the belief that just eating raw will cleanse and detoxify the body over a period of time. I think this statement may have some validity, but why not get the body balanced first by adhering to "The Rules of the Stomach," and then rebuild with a predominantly raw cuisine? What I've learned from my own experience is that it is not so much the foods we might combine improperly as it is the ratio and relationship of various food groups that can have the adverse effects on digestion and absorption. For instance, it is not recommended to eat fruits and vegetables at the same meal. Eat your fruits first and wait at least half an hour before eating the vegetables. I often will include a little lemon or lime juice in my recipes for salad dressings and entrees, or add a little chopped fruit to a salad for flavor or color. This usually will be small in relationship to the whole.

It is the quantity here that is the determining factor. It is very small in relationship to the rest of the ingredients and thus does not seem to be a problem.

13

Categories
for Food Combining

Proteins

Raw-food proteins include seeds, avocadoes, and nuts. Legumes and grains do contain some protein but they are considered starches for the purpose of food combining, as starch is the predominant element in these foods. It is not recommended that starches and proteins be eaten at the same time, as they require different digestive environments to break down the food. Proteins do combine well with vegetables, with the exception of the starchy-type vegetables such as corn, potatoes, carrots, etc. They also combine well with fermented foods such as seed cheeses, raw crackers, and sauerkrauts.

Starches

Starches include the legumes and grains mentioned above, along with corn, artichokes, winter squash, peas, carrots, beets, potatoes, yams, sweet potatoes, and jicama. Starches combine well with vegetables but not with proteins. They do combine well with the fermented foods.

Vegetables

The array of raw vegetable possibilities is vast, including sprouts, lettuces, spinach, onions, garlic, ginger, cabbage, and all the crucifers like cauliflower, broccoli, Brussels sprouts, kale, collard greens, and bok choy. The cruciferous vegetables, by the way, are very high in antioxidants and are wonderful preventatives of cancer. Vegetables combine well with proteins or starches but not with fruits.

Fruits

These are your sweet fruits, sub-acid fruits, and acid fruits. Sweet fruits include bananas and all dried fruits such as dates and raisins. These are high in sugar, and if you have any kind of sugar imbalance it is best to minimize or leave these foods alone. The acid fruits are citrus, pineapples, and strawberries; sub-acid fruits include apples, pears, papayas, kiwi, etc.

Fruits should always be eaten alone and not combined with vegetables, proteins, or starches. Acid fruits and sub-acid fruits combine well, and sub-acid and sweet fruits combine well, but acid fruits and sweet fruits usually are not compatible. Melons are in a category of their own for the purpose of food combining, because these fruits very high water content will pass through the stomach quickly (approximately 30 minutes) if not poorly combined, i.e., if eaten alone on an empty stomach. Melons are generally high in sugar but abundant in enzymes and have wonderful cleansing properties. It is best to eat these by themselves so that you can benefit from all that they have to offer. Watermelons have the highest water content and really should be eaten first, before any other fruit or melons.

Water

Although water is rarely considered a food, it is essential to our health and should never be consumed with any other meal or food. Water is often served at meals but if we drink water with our meals (or any liquids for that matter), we dilute the digestive enzymes needed to break down our food, ending up with indigestion and poor absorption. Drink your water and liquids alone before your meals, or wait a good hour after your meal.

Fermented Foods

Fermented raw foods have wonderful rejuvenating properties. They are full of enzymes and the good friendly bacteria necessary to help break down the body's wastes in the large intestine and help produce certain nutrients like vitamin B12. These foods also aid digestion. The fermented foods in this recipe book include the seed cheeses (made from nuts and seeds), sauerkraut, crackers, breads, and rejuvelac. Rejuvelac is an amazing drink that is full of B vitamins, enzymes, and acidophilus bifidus (friendly intestinal flora). It is used as a starter for the seed cheeses and as a drink to reestablish the friendly bacteria in the intestinal tract.

Food
Combining for Optimum Digestion

It is not recommended that starches and proteins be combined at the same meal. Starches require a more alkaline pH and proteins a more acidic pH in the stomach to break them down. If you eat these together you get the same effect as you would if you added vinegar to baking soda—a gastronomical explosion resulting in heartburn, acid refluxes, putrefaction, fermentation, and eventual breakdown of the system.

If we sprout our nuts and seeds, legumes and grains, they then move into the vegetable category for the purpose of proper food combining. I usually soak or sprout my grains, nuts, and seeds before using them in my recipes. They combine better and are so much easier to digest, not to mention the abundance of enzymes that it activates and the enhanced nutrition that results. More on sprouting later.

1. Drink your liquids alone.
2. Eat melons alone or leave them alone. Eat watermelon by itself or at least fifteen minutes before other melons at the same meal.
3. Eat fruits alone.
4. Acid and sub-acid fruits are okay together, and sub-acid and sweet fruits are okay, but do not combine acid and sweet fruits.
5. Do not combine proteins and starches unless sprouted first.
6. Proteins and vegetables are okay.
7. Starches and vegetables are okay.
8. Fermented foods combine well with vegetables, proteins, and starches because they are made from sprouted nuts, seeds, and/or grains.

If you would like more information on food combining, there are many books available that you can access through nutritionist David Wolfe's website: www.davidwolfe.com or through www.rawfood.com. Or you can purchase videos and tapes from the store at the Optimum Health Institute (see Resources list).

Rules of the **Stomach**

 Why Water?

Water is vital to hydrate the cells of our body. Like a battery, the body will not hold a charge unless the cells are well hydrated. Water is also very oxygenating to our body, as water is one-third oxygen.

Water is an important component in the production of the mucous linings of the digestive tract in order for digestion to be optimal. It helps the body to neutralize and eliminate toxins. Water is synonymous with life itself, as our bodies are more than 70 percent water. The amount and quality of water we get is so important to our ability to sustain and nourish the life of the human body. We need to keep that balance. The book titled *Your Body's Many Cries for Water* is a wonderful piece of reading material to give you more detailed information on why to drink plenty of water. It is recommended that you drink eight to twelve 8-ounce glasses of water each day.

Science is now proving that water has the amazing ability to hold and transmit information, such as in homeopathic medicine. Since our bodies are mostly water it becomes very important to entertain positive thoughts and positive affirmations to ourselves, because our mental states are constantly in interaction with our water makeup, which is in constant contact with all our cells. Just as food provides nutrition to our bodies, our thoughts provide information to our cells. With focused intention and positive affirmations we can transform the health of the physical body. See the books *The Living Energy Universe* and *The Hidden Messages in Water,* as well as the website www.trivortex.com for more information.

It is at this time that I want to interject the importance of preparing food with a loving attitude. LOVE is an essential nutrient and one that has the most powerful healing effect on the body. When meals are prepared with love, the body can sense it, and even though the ingredients may not be of the highest quality or the best in health, the vibration and intention of love in the food is transmitted and received by every cell in the body. As explained clearly in *The Living Energy Universe, The Holographic Universe,* and *Power vs.*

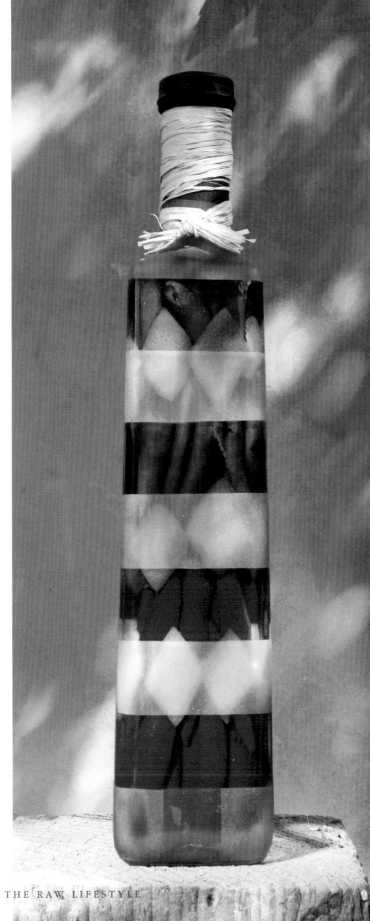

> ### *Love*
> *is an essential nutrient and one that has the most powerful healing effect on the body.*

Force (see Recommend Reading list), everything—every word, thought, and deed—is recorded and connected to everything else in the Universe. This is no longer simply a New Age concept; it is receiving more and more scientific validation. As you prepare the following recipes with love, that ingredient will become a part of all who share in your meals.

Fats, Proteins, Sugars, and Starches

Fats

Fats are necessary for the functioning of the body and may be compared to the lubrication system of an automobile. They keep things smoothly "oiled" and give us a protective covering around our organs, tissues, and nerves. Fats are made up of glycerin and fatty acids; the quantity and kinds of fatty acids attached to the glycerin molecule determine the fat type.

Essential fatty acids are fats that the body cannot manufacture, so to obtain them we must depend on our foods. These are found in raw plant fatty foods such as avocadoes, nuts, and seeds. Essential fatty acids (EFAs) are destroyed with heat; thus they are not found in cooked foods. Actually, all natural fats when heated turn into trans fatty acids that are unrecognizable by the body and so are beyond the body's ability to break them down. These substances turn into strings of fatty tissue that adhere to the inside of veins and arteries. This leads to degenerative diseases.

It is important to purchase your fats (oils) cold-pressed or expelled and to refrigerate them ASAP. Raw plant fats have no cholesterol in them. They assist in the delivery of minerals to the cells. Your raw plant fats are full of the lipase enzyme, which helps in the digestion of these fats and the break-down of stored fat in the fat cells. Cooked fats by contrast add nothing to our health and are a major source of damaging free radicals. Being lipase-deficient, they are hard to digest, and they interfere with the cells' ability to exchange oxygen and nutrients. Cooking fats of any kind also congeals the red blood cells, causing them to clump together and create sluggishness in the lymphatic system, circulatory system, and respiratory system. They are nutri-ent-deficient and add unwanted weight to the body.

The raw plant fats are wonderful antioxidants and protect the body from pollution, lubricate the delicate mucous lining of the digestive system, and help in the production of hormones. They help us to metabolize stagnated

Understanding these foods is basic to finding balance and transforming our health.

fats that have built up in the body from eating cooked fats. The liver easily recognizes raw plant fats, unlike the cooked trans fatty acids that clog our arteries and weaken the cell membranes, thereby allowing other substances into the cell that can damage them.

When moving to a more raw diet or vegetarian diet, some people feel they need to eat more proteins to fill that empty space left by eliminating animal protein foods. What the body really wants is F A T—the right kinds of fat.

Coconut oil is far superior to other fats. In the past coconut oil got a bad rap, but research is finding that it reduces the risk of arteriosclerosis, cancer, and other degenerative diseases; prevents bacterial, viral, and fungal infections; aids the body in fighting viruses of various kinds; supports the immune system; helps prevent osteoporosis and diabetes; promotes weight loss, improves digestion, keeps the skin soft and smooth, and many other benefits. I won't elaborate on the "hows" here but invite you to read The Healing Miracles of Coconut Oil (see Recommended Reading list).

The next best oil is raw flax oil with its abundance of the essential fatty acids, omega-6 and omega-3. Olive oils are good also but best when stone-pressed, cold-pressed, or expelled and purchased as extra virgin. All oils must be kept in the fridge after opening, or they will accelerate in their rancidity.

In my recipes I use mostly organic olive oils that are cold-pressed and extra virgin. Extra virgin olive oils do have a distinct flavor, so please take that into consideration with what you are making and use a lighter olive oil if it seems appropriate. The very best olive oil you can purchase is the stoned ground olive oil that Rawfood.com sells, see the Resources list.

Proteins

Proteins are composed of amino acid chains and need an acidic environment in the stomach for digestion to occur. If we are eating large molecules of cooked proteins then it will take much longer to digest these foods. Furthermore, the cooking process "denatures" the protein (alters the molecule). This is not an optimum form of protein, and often it won't get properly digested. In the cooking

process many of the amino acids get destroyed. Cooked proteins such as animal flesh, inorganic dairy products, cheeses, etc., have high quantities of toxic chemicals in them along with artificial hormones. These foods can be quite inflammatory and eventually lead to many major diseases.

The best forms of proteins (amino acids) are found in your green leafy vegetables, wild weeds, sprouted nuts, seeds, grains, and legumes. Wheatgrass juice (See section on cleansing, next) is a wonderful source of protein and a very powerful cleanser and detoxifier for the body.

When we sprout our nuts and seeds it takes much less energy and enzyme activity to break down the loosened peptide bonds that hold the amino acids in place. They are then a lot easier to digest and assimilate.

Sugars

Refined sugar is a drug, and there is no way to get around this. It causes artificial highs, depression, mood swings, and energy crashes. It was used as a recreational drug back in the sixteenth century in the royal courts of Europe. Like the poppy seed goes through different stages of processing to become heroin, sugar cane or sugar beets are processed to become that white powder we call sugar. Sugar is a great stress on the pancreas, which struggles to balance the blood sugar levels with insulin. The average Amer-

Refined sugar is a drug and there is no way to get around this.

ican eats between 100 and 150 pounds of sugar a year, if you can imagine that. The largest sugar consumption is in sodas by teenagers. There is up to 16 teaspoons of sugar in each can of soda pop. This is devastating to the body because sugar can create an acid condition. When the body is acidic it will try to neutralize its acids by drawing the alkaline minerals out of the bones, leaving the body demineralized. Sugar destroys B vitamins, creates problems with digestion, and enlarges the liver (as seen with the sugar in alcohol). It feeds parasites, *Candida,* and cancer. It adds calories without nutrition, slows the metabolism by affecting the thyroid gland, and weakens the immune system. Refined white sugar ferments in the system, causing the formation of acetic acid, carbonic acid, and alcohol, which will eventually add to the breakdown of the system.

Starches and Carbohydrates

These foods are made up of a long chain of glucose molecules and break down relatively slowly in the body (as compared to fruits, vegetables, and simple sugars). They are considered a more complex glucose molecule than sugar, even though starches and carbohydrates eventually break down into simpler glucose sugar molecules and can have effects on the body similar to the more refined sugars.

Hybridized starches—especially ones like wheat, rice, soy, corn, potatoes, carrots, beets, and seedless starchy fruits—are all higher in sugar and lower in minerals than their organic counterparts, and many of them are genetically altered. It is always best to try to buy organic produce.

When advising others who have decided to transform to optimum health, I usually suggest a cleansing program first, then a rebuilding program to follow. A deep cleansing program is made up of fresh squeezed juices and lighter raw foods. I suggest leaving the heavier fatty foods and oils for later.

It is always best to prepare the body by first eliminating the foods that are debilitating and acidic to the system. These include coffee, ice cream, and all of the white foods like white flour, white sugar, white milk, etc. You can do this over a period of time so that your body can get used to not having these foods and can detox gradually.

Cleansing sometimes can be uncomfortable as the accumulated toxins start to release from the body. One may experience tiredness, irritability, cravings, nausea, dizziness, and/or itching. These are all normal detox symptoms. After these more deleterious foods are eliminated then do a couple of days on just fruits, juices, and vegetables with perhaps some of the seed cheeses. After this, one can fast for a few days on juices. Three days is what I suggest. A supervising professional in this field and a doctor's permission are highly recommended (almost essential) for longer periods of fasting.

How a fast is broken is very important, and I suggest it be followed by a cleansing raw-food diet until the tongue is pink upon waking in the morning. This is a good indicator of the body having finished its detoxification process. For juices, I recommend a combination of cucumber, kale, and celery as these are very alkaline to the body and will neutralize excess acidity. There are many other wonderful juice combinations, and I invite you to refer to a book called *Juicing for Life* (see Recommended Reading) to learn many creative and healing ways to combine your fruits and vegetables. I have incorporated some of these recipes in the section on juices.

Wheatgrass juice is the most powerful detoxifier there is. Its nutritional components far exceed any other food—for example, it is a rich source of protein, calcium, potassium, and magnesium. Magnesium is considered "the antidepressant mineral." On a more spiritual level, I truly believe that wheatgrass juice is an evolutionary food that can accelerate the de-densification of the mind-body connection. With its high vibrational quality it can raise the vibration of our cells as it throws off the toxic materials and then subsequently raises the vibrational quality of our thoughts and emotions. When cleansing, especially for the first time, it is recommended that one do a series of colonics or enemas to help keep the colon clean while releasing stored toxins from the tissues and bloodstream. This will speed up the process of detoxification, and soon you will start to feel the benefits of eating cleansing raw foods that give you an abundance of energy and a feeling of well-being.

When I was working at the Optimum Health Institute in California, I frequently saw amazing results in people's health by the end of their first week. I have personally witnessed guests arriving pushing a walker, and after only two weeks of cleansing the body, they are literally running up the stairs. I've heard testimony after testimony about the miracles that people can experience by going through a cleansing program. I invite you to look up the Optimum Health Institute in Lemon Grove—it's a place you can go for a retreat that supports your body to cleanse and return to balance. Their website is www.optimumhealth.org. See also Rawfood.com

for retreats (Resources list).

I have included in these pages many recipes that would be suitable for a cleansing program. They are the ones with no oils, very little avocado (if any), and none of the heavier nuts and seeds. The best nuts and seeds to use when cleansing are your sunflower, sesame, pumpkin, and pine nuts, and they must always be soaked (germinated). In my recipes try to substitute a more cleansing seed if it calls for a heavier nut or seed.

Be watchful of overdoing the fruits, and stay away from the dried fruits and starchy fruits like bananas while cleansing. These will raise the blood sugar levels rapidly, possibly creating more cravings for other foods. Part of cleansing and detoxing is breaking our addiction to sugars, so go easy on the carrots and beets, especially if juicing them, as they are also high in sugars. When cleansing, make sure that you are drinking plenty of water and combining your foods according to the Rules of the Stomach (see Food Combining section).

Breathing

Since we are talking about transformation and health, we must not fail to mention the importance of our breath. It is our link to the life force itself (Prana=Spirit). Without breath we could not live in a body.

I have been working with the breath for more than twenty-five years. I have facilitated thousands of people in breath work, and it never ceases to amaze me how unbelievably powerful the breath is and how transforming it can be. I'm sure that most of us have heard the many benefits of breathing exercises and the benefits of oxygenation to the cells. Our level of vitality and health does not depend solely on what kinds of foods we eat but also on how we breathe or don't breathe. The air we breathe today has considerably less nutrients than it had thousands of years ago. What does that mean to us? We have to work harder to get the oxygen we need. Cancers and all degenerative diseases will proliferate in an oxygen-deficient environment. We wonder why cancer is epidemic today.

Researchers state that we use only about 20 percent of our lung capacity. That percentage along with the air quality and the food quality can greatly affect our state of health or disease.

Past trauma, repressed or suppressed emotions, social conditioning, negative thinking and beliefs, judgments, fashion (tight clothing), stress, etc., all can close off our breath until one day we realize that we can hardly take a deep breath without feeling faint or dizzy. Breath work can be an amazing tool to transform these issues and once again open the breath, allowing an increase in oxygen to the cells and a deeper connection to our Higher Self.

You might ask how the breath can do all that-and don't we breathe all the time? In conscious breath work, we breathe with an intention to bring in more joy. A high vibrational frequency is created at a cellular level that transforms negative or lower vibrational patterns stored in the subconscious mind.

Researchers
state that we use only
about 20 percent of
our lung capacity.

This happens through the physics principle of entrainment, which states that a lower-frequency pattern of energy will entrain to a higher-frequency pattern. These lower-frequency patterns of negative or repressed energy will integrate into the higher-frequency pattern, which is created by a specific breathing pattern. As we release and integrate these negative energies we can then access expanded states of awareness, increasing the vibrational quality of our lives, our health, and our experience.

Breath work has many benefits. It has the ability to change our mental and emotional states, bring the physical body back into balance, clear toxins, kill pathogens and cancer cells, improve heart conditions, strengthen the immune system, improve the lymphatic, digestive, and circulatory systems, and reestablish the link between the physical body and the Spiritual body. It is truly something to experience. I invite you to attend a breathing workshop in your area and to read Judy Kravitz's book, *Breathe Deep, Laugh Loudly* (see Recommended Reading list). To access workshops or seminars you can search the Internet under "breath work" or visit my website at www.Transform2000.com.

Yoga and Exercise

When talking about transformation for optimum health, raw living foods cannot be the only element of our program. We must not

Yoga has amazing health benefits.

forget exercise as a daily routine or at least three times a week for thirty minutes or more. Exercise should consist of a cardiovascular routine that works the heart and lungs, like swimming, dancing, or fast walking, and an easier stretching and breathing exercise like yoga. Yoga increases flexibility while building strength and endurance. Yoga means union-the union of the mind, body, and spirit. It is a philosophy of life that encompasses many aspects. One aspect of yoga is a comprehensive series of stretching movements that utilizes the breath and focuses on opening up restrictions in the musculature of the body. It is a full mind-body exercise that anyone can do at any level of flexibility. There are many books written on yoga (see Recommended Reading for a sample of titles).

Yoga has amazing health benefits. It is the only exercise that I know of whereby with practice we can get better at it with age. It increases our flexibility, endurance, and muscle strength. It improves circulation, concentration, respiration, the elimination of toxins and wastes, and much more. It is rejuvenative and regenerative and can help us to connect more deeply with our Higher Self, thus making yoga another tool for personal transformation.

Meditation

Meditation is an awareness trance in which we retract from the outside world and go inside to our inner world. Meditation is a concentrated focus on one thought, object, sound, or idea. It has the effect of calming the mental chatter and allowing the brainwave pattern to slow down. Through this practice we come to a place of being aware that there is an observer Self, a silent witness to the mental activity of one's mind. Through meditation we come to identify more with

this awareness, this place of pure consciousness and peace. It is through this connection that transformation happens for us and we become more detached from our thoughts, resulting in more peace, clarity, creativity, and enlightenment.

Quantum Healing

Before leaving Part I of this book I want to mention the rapidly growing technology in bio-energetic medicine. Refer to the Recommended Reading list for books and websites on bio-energetic medicine. Bioenergetics or vibrational medicine has been around for eons and is the premise upon which acupuncture and homeopathy is built. This field

is expanding at great speed, as we can now interface energetic fields with a computer and use the latter to make swift and much more accurate readings on electrical measurements than ever before. Now the world's most advanced biofeedback can be obtained with a bioenergetics device available on the open market; it is called the QXCI/SCIO device. This advanced biofeedback mechanism can evaluate what is going on with the mind-body connection, as well as balance the body using energetic treatments from a variety of modalities.

This device can detect internal and external stresses on the body such as pathogens (parasites, bacteria, fungus, *Candida,* etc.), allergies, nutritional deficiencies or excesses, organ and system weaknesses, stress, hereditary pre-dispositions, diseases, mental and emotional disorders that can affect the physical body, and many others. Once these are identified, the device can then stimulate an energetic pattern to help bring the body back into balance. I have been working with this technology for a few years now, and I believe it is truly the medicine of the future. We are becoming more aware that we are an energetic field, and one that can be measured and balanced energetically.

I use the QXCI/SCIO to monitor my health and to let me know when I need to do a cleansing fast or which foods are best for me to eat. I can even test certain foods to see if they are compatible with me, and whether or not the foods are organic or genetically modified. I can energize my drinking water and be notified when I'm deficient in certain nutrients. It has also made me aware of the mental and emotional issues I have that may exert an adverse effect on my physical body. The best part to all of this is that the QXCI/SCIO can bring these areas back into balance by selecting the appropriate ener-getic treatments. To gain more information on this you can access the website at www.quantumalternative.com. Also I invite you to read "The Promorpheus" by Dr. William C. Nelson, the inventor of this device. His website is www.qxsubspace.com. There you will find extensive information about this technology and his book.

Part 2

Food Preparation Basics

Getting Started

The first step is setting up the kitchen to support your new lifestyle and purchasing the necessary stock ingredients and appliances for making these recipes.

Having the basic ingredients on hand makes these recipes easy and appetizing. If you are missing one or even two ingredients then try to substitute with something else. This is often how new recipes are created. In buying spices or nuts and seeds I always seek and recommend organic, although at times this may not be practical so just do your best. Following are some simple suggestions for spices and foods to stock your pantry and get you started with a raw-foods lifestyle.

It is best to store nuts, seeds, beans, and grains in glass and keep them in a cool, dark place, rotating them as you use them. If you buy larger quantities of nuts and seeds then it is best to refrigerate or put them in the freezer until ready to use. This will help preserve their freshness. You may find one or two ingredients in my recipes that are not one hundred percent pure and raw, but I have done my best to minimize this discrepancy, so if this is a problem for you, then just omit the ingredient.

Ingredients

Spices

Oregano, Basil, Ginger, Thyme, Mustard, Cilantro, Cayenne, Caraway seed, Mustard seed, Tomato powder, Celtic sea salt, Dill, Onion powder, Miso (a fermented soybean paste), Dulse, Parsley, Curry, Kelp, Garlic powder, Cumin, Chili powder, Cinnamon, Nutmeg.

Flavorings

Bragg's Liquid Aminos (this is a low-sodium type of soya sauce found in health food stores), Nama Shoyu (this is a soya sauce used quite often in Asian recipes), Vanilla extract, Coconut extract, Almond extract, Pineapple extract (these are flavorings used mostly in desserts).

Nuts

Almonds, Cashews, Hazelnuts, Pecans, Pine nuts, Walnuts, Macadamia nuts, Brazil nuts.

Seeds

Flax seeds, Sunflower seeds, Sesame seeds, Pumpkin seeds.

Oils

Extra-virgin cold-pressed or stone-ground olive oil, flax oil.

Nut Butters

Cashew Butter, Almond Butter, Raw Tahini.

Dried Fruits

Dates, Raisins, Apricots, Mangos, Currants, Pineapple, Peaches, Coconut, Apricots (Turkish are the best).

Grains

Rye, Wheat, Quinoa, Wild rice, Buckwheat.

Sea Vegetables

Dulse, Kelp, Nori sheets.

Fresh Fruits

Stay with what is in season. I like to have on hand fresh oranges, lemon, bananas (fresh and frozen for smoothies), apples, papayas, avocados, and coconuts. If I have fruits that are getting too ripe then I'll freeze them for smoothies, or dehydrate them. You can purchase other fruits as needed according to what you are making.

Fresh Vegetables

Keep these on hand on a regular basis and buy others as needed: lettuces, baby greens, tomatoes, carrots, celery, onions, garlic,

cucumbers, cabbage, basil, green onions, beets. I find that with a raw-food lifestyle I discard very little, as I will freeze, dehydrate, or juice anything that looks like it's getting tired. These will have less nutrient value than their fresh counterpart but it does eliminate waste.

I like to keep some seeds soaked and available in my refrigerator so I have them on hand to whip up an entree or dressing or just to munch. I suggest having sunflower seeds and almonds on hand and ready to go. These can be soaked and then stored in the fridge in water. (See the section on soaking and sprouting.) Remember to change the water daily when storing in this fashion. This will prolong the shelf life of these foods.

It is best to make this transition gradually, so as you start to clean out your kitchen of the superfluous items, you can replace them with the ones you like. If you can start with implementing one new recipe a day into your life, pretty soon you will be transforming in the raw, living a high raw-food lifestyle.

Make it fun and enjoyable!

Make it fun and enjoyable, colorful and flavorful as you transition from the old to the new.

Kitchen
Equipment

Get started now.

To facilitate implementation of the raw and living foods lifestyle you will need certain appliances and equipment. You can use what you have on hand and slowly add to your inventory. The most important appliance will be a Champion Juicer, Sampson Juicer, or Green Power or Green Life Juicer. I prefer the Champion myself as I find it easier to use, with less parts to wash, and greater speed in moving foods through the hopper. Often you can find these juicers second-hand at garage sales for less than a hundred dollars. More on juices below.

You will need a good strong blender and food processor and a food dehydrator, although your oven at a very low temperature with the door ajar could suffice initially. Another option if you are living in a hot sunny climate is to dehydrate in the sun using a screen to shield the food from bugs.

If you choose this latter method then make sure there is sufficient air ventilation around the food. If you don't have a juicer you can purchase fresh-squeezed juice at a juice bar, and they may even give you vegetable pulp if that is something you need.

Get started now and gradually add what you need as you go along.

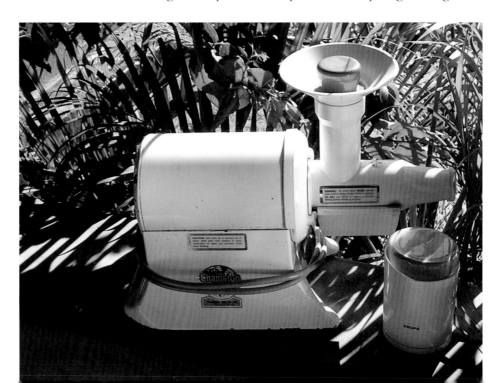

Blender

The average household blender is less powerful than the Vita-Mix, but it is a common appliance that we all have in our kitchen and one that can get us started until we can purchase the Vita-Mix. (See Resources list.)

Blenders are useful for making the seed milks, smoothies, purees, pesto, dressings, and soups. Costs can vary between $30 and $60.

Champion Juicer

This is a fine juicer that I would not like to be without. It is a masticating juicer that grinds the vegetables into a fine pulp, squeezing the juice out and expelling the pulp. It is a continuous-feed juicer, so you don't have to stop and clean it like you would with the centrifugal-style ones. It has a "blank" attachment or solid plastic piece that when inserted instead of the juicing screen can make pâtés, nut butters, ice creams, sherbets, coconut creams, and vegetable pulps. The Champion comes in a home model as well as an industrial-strength model. Both are excellent but I prefer the heavy-duty one, as I am constantly working with it and making meals for larger groups of people. This juicer should last a

lifetime, and the parts are replaceable and easy to get.

Citrus Juicer

This appliance comes in very handy for juicing oranges or lemons. You can find these in any discount department store for about $15.

Coffee Grinder

A small coffee grinder is wonderful for grinding up small quantities of spices, nuts, seeds, or dehydrated veggies. I just use the one I had when I used to grind up coffee beans.

Colander

This is a large strainer, preferably with a long handle, useful for draining and rinsing sprouts, nuts, and seeds, or washing certain vegetables.

Dehydrator

The dehydrator works like an oven and is useful for making all kinds of raw dehydrated snacks, crackers, breads, burgers, appetizers, desserts, pizzas, casseroles, etc. The best is the Excalibur, and it comes in three sizes. For two people the medium size is best. It has a thermostat so you can regulate the temperature not to exceed the 105-degree limit necessary for preserving the enzymes. There are many other kinds of dehydrator out there, but this is the best. Other dehydrators do not dry the foods evenly. (See Resources list.)

Garlic Press

This is a common item that most people will already have in their kitchen. It is useful in pressing garlic and ginger and mashing it to a fine pulp. You can also use the fine grater teeth on a typical grater for this purpose if you don't have a garlic press.

Green Power Juicer

This is a more sophisticated juicer than the Champion and will do everything the Champion does plus juice wheatgrass. We discussed wheatgrass in a previous section, and I wouldn't be without some way to juice it for the times when I'm doing a cleanse or a fast. This machine will help you avoid having to purchase an additional juicer for wheatgrass alone. The Green Power Juicer is said to be superior in preserving enzymes and nutrients, as it operates at a lower speed and thus does not heat up.

Knives

You will need an assortment of knives for chopping, slicing, and mincing your foods. Make sure that the knives are sharpened regularly and are of good quality.

Mandolin

A mandolin is a slicing tool. I recommend the low-priced home-use mandolin for slicing or grating fruits and veggies into various textures and shapes. This utensil is a must for making the lasagna noodles or raw bacon.

Saladacco

I think the name of this gadget has changed now to Joyce Chen. This hand-held utensil creates an angel-hair spaghetti-like thread from hard vegetables. This is great for making "pasta" dishes with root veggies and squashes. It also has a setting for making spirals that are nice for garnishing.

Saladshooter

This small, hand-held appliance slices or grates vegetables, fruits, nuts, and seeds. It has various blades for different purposes. Although it is easy to use and clean, I find that with my regular grater and food processor, the saladshooter is not an essential item.

Salad Spinner

This is essential if you are washing your lettuces and greens for salads just before serving (i.e., without time for the greens to air-dry). This utensil spins greens dry using centrifugal force. When our greens are dry the dressings adhere to them much better.

Sprout Bags

These fine-mesh bags (usually nylon) can be purchased at health food stores. The Optimum Health Institute sells them for about $2.95 each. They may be called seed bags or sprout bags, but make sure they are not the heavy hemp kind. In addition to sprouting certain seeds, these bags are useful in making the seed cheeses.

Vita-Mix

Once you get hooked on raw, this will become a must-have item for your kitchen. This heavy-duty blender will last a lifetime. I like it because if it gets over-heated or strained from too much food in the blender then it will shut off automatically and restart in about fifteen minutes. It is great for making soups, seed cheeses, pâtés, smoothies, and all the other things that you would normally use your blender for. You can even warm up soups in them by blending for a longer period of time but remember that the longer you blend anything, the more oxidation you create, with a resulting loss of nutrients. (See Resources list to order.)

Wheatgrass Juicer

This appliance is essential for the times you want to do a fast, cleanse, or just juice wheatgrass and drink (ideally on a regular basis). The taste of wheatgrass is not one that I espe-cially look forward to, so I use wheatgrass more medicinally than as an everyday food. There are many models, but I find that the small one from Optimum Health Institute works just fine and takes up very little space. (See Resources list.)

As a general rule, I will not eat a seed, nut, or grain without first soaking and/or sprouting it. When we soak nuts and seeds we are basically starting the germination process. These nuts and seeds have been sitting dormant, waiting for the right environment to start growing. When we soak these foods at room temperature we are giving the signal for these seeds to start growing. In the dormant stage a seed has enzyme inhibitors to preserve and protect it. As we soak it, the enzyme inhibitors are released and the enzymes are activated. The seed springs to life and is charged with an abundance of life force, enzymes, and nutrients. Often by soaking seeds we can double, triple, and sometimes quadruple the nutrient content of the seed. Soaking will also help to diminish some of the fat content and will help convert the dense vegetable protein to simpler amino acids for easier digestion. The more complex carbohydrates in the foods will also start to break down into the simpler glucose molecules. We can see from this that soaking and sprouting our nuts, seeds, and grains has many benefits—from more enzymes, nutrients, and life force to easier digestion and less fat.

Try to remember that when you soak a seed it will swell and sometimes double or triple in size. So make sure that there is plenty of water to cover them. In the following recipes the quantities are stated as either dry or soaked for measurement purposes. I include a soaking and sprouting chart for soaking times, harvesting times, and yields. What I have found for myself is that it can be quite complicated following these charts, so I tend to just soak everything overnight unless it is a larger seed or legume like almonds and chickpeas, which I will soak at least two days. When soaking, always use purified water.

For rinsing, tap water will suffice. When soaking for longer periods, remember to change the water at least twice a day. This will also apply if storing seeds in the refrigerator.

For soaking it's best to use a bowl or jar, and I prefer to use glass. After you

Sprouting
actives
enzymes.

42

have soaked your seeds you are ready to sprout them.

For sprouting it is important to rinse your soaked seeds with fresh tap water and then place them in a sprouting jar or sprouting tray, making sure that there is ventilation and the temperature is not above 80 degrees. I have found that in hotter climates the seeds will tend to mold or wilt. I recently heard that spraying vinegar on them after rinsing will prevent this, but I have yet to try that theory out.

You can make your own sprout jar by using a wide-mouth Mason preserving jar and wrapping some nylon screen over the top, securing it with an elastic band. Tilt your jars at a 45-degree angle and place in the dish rack so that the water from your seeds after rinsing can drain properly, and the jar has good ventilation. I will sometimes place a tea towel over my jars initially to keep the seeds in a darkened environment. They seem to like this in the first stages of the sprouting process. You could also place your seeds in a darkened cupboard, sitting on an angle with a tray to catch the water. My experience with this is that it's easy to forget to rinse them when they are not in sight. I have found some interesting-looking specimens days later after forgetting that I had put them there.

It is best to refer to the charts for harvesting times. Of course, if you want to eat a sprout before full fruition then go ahead. That really is a personal preference and may be what is needed for a specific recipe. Those sprouts that contain chlorophyll like alfalfa and clover will need to be exposed to indirect sunlight so that they can convert the sunlight to chlorophyll. Never put them in direct sunlight.

Harvesting and Storage

For nuts, seeds, and grains that are to be used after soaking you just need to rinse and they are ready for use. There are a couple of exceptions. When flax seeds are soaked they will double in size and form a gelatinous substance that is almost impossible to rinse off and really is unnecessary for most uses. I will strain the soaked flax seed in a large colander, leaving it to drain over the sink for about five minutes, and then I use the seeds. Flax is very gelatinous; when strained the gel makes a great facial mask if you collect it in a bowl as it drains. The gel has many nutrients that will feed your skin, and it helps to tighten the pores.

The other seed that is an exception to the "simply soak and rinse" rule is the sunflower. This is a most versatile seed and one I use often for seed cheeses, dressings, and more. When sunflower seeds are soaked they will double in size and shed a thin translucent shell that floats to the top of the bowl. To remove these I turn on the hot water tap in my kitchen sink and while rinsing I very gently massage the sunflower seeds to help loosen any remaining skins. As these surface they can easily be removed by gently skimming off the top with your palm or tilting the bowl and allowing them to run off into the sink. Repeat this procedure two or three times. Your drained bowl of washed and rinsed sunflower seeds is ready to use.

They can also be stored in the fridge by covering with water. This is an ideal way to prolong the shelf life of anything that has been previously soaked. Remember to change the water daily and try to use the food as soon as possible. To store harvested and sprouted grains, seeds, or legumes I prefer the "Ever-Fresh Green Bags" that are designed to preserve freshness and extend shelf life. They can be bought from the Optimum Health Institute Store and come in a variety of sizes. Sprouted lentils, mung beans, or other small legumes are fine in a Tupperware-style container and then refrigerated. Always smell your sprouts before using to make sure that they have not gone bad.

Sprouting in Soil

Sowing seeds or grains in a tray of soil is an entirely different way to sprout and will produce a much different kind of sprout. We call these "sprouts" but really they are more like young green shoots. The most common green shoots or sprouts are the buckwheat greens, the sunflower greens, and wheatgrass.

When buying the seeds for these, make sure that you buy both sunflower and buckwheat with the shells on. Sunflower seeds with shells come in a variety of colors from black to gray with dark stripes. The buckwheat seeds usually have a black shell. For wheatgrass, I like to use the hard winter wheat berry seed. All these seeds will need to be soaked for 24 hours to start the germination process. (Change the water after 12 hours to ensure that the seeds are soaking in nice clean water.) Then rinse the seeds and let them sprout for another 12–24 hours. This stage is not always necessary and sometimes I will go right to the next stage.

To plant, you first need to prepare the soil. I use a shallow planting tray, which can be purchased at any garden center or nursery. They are about two feet square by three inches deep. I put approximately one inch of dirt or organic potting soil in a tray and level it out, so that it's even. Then I sprinkle my seeds lightly and evenly over the top surface. Next, I water carefully, trying not to disturb the even distribution. I then place another tray inverted on top of the planted tray to create a housing for the young sprouts to grow, and to keep them warm and protected from birds or insects that may want to feast on the young greens. I water twice a day until the shoots are about an inch or so in height, then I remove the top tray and expose them to indirect sunlight. I grow my sprouts in my greenhouse but know many people who have great success growing trays of seeds indoors.

Wheatgrass is ready for harvesting when it is about four to five inches high. I use scissors or a serrated knife to cut the greens just above the base of the plant. Wheatgrass is one of the most powerful detoxifying foods on the planet. Also, at times of year when fresh greens are scarce, then a shot or two of wheatgrass juice each day seems to give the body all the nutrients it needs.

The sunflower greens are best harvested when about the same size in height (4–5 inches) and when the leaves have a rich, full (almost meaty) appearance and taste. These make a wonderful addition to tossed green salads or sprout salads and are full of enzymes and all the vitamins from A to Z.

Buckwheat greens are harvestable when all the black shells have fallen off (or the majority of them). You may have to pick some of these out later after you wash and drain the cut shoots. Usually they will grow to be about five inches in height. They remind me of little four-leaf clover sprouts that I used to find in the fields when I was a kid. These are so delicious and full of calcium, enzymes, and vitamin K. They make a wonderful filling for the sushi rolls and wraps. See the Resources list at the back for ordering information.

Amount	Nut, Seed, Legume, or Grain	Soaking Time	Sprouting Time	Yield
1 cup	Adzuki beans	12 hrs	3–5 days	4 cups
3 Tbs	Alfalfa	5 hrs	4–6 days	3–4 cups
1 cup	Almonds	12–15 hrs	1 day	1¾ cups
1 cup	Brazil nuts	8 hr		⅛ cup
2 Tbs	Broccoli seed	8 hrs	3–4 days	2 cups
1 cup	Buckwheat, hulled	12–15 hrs	1–3 days	2–3 cups
3 cups	Buckwheat, unhulled	12–15 hrs	7–9 days	one tray

Note: 3 cups of buckwheat, unhulled, will produce approximately one tray of greens.

Amount	Nut, Seed, Legume, or Grain	Soaking Time	Sprouting Time	Yield
3 Tbs	Clover Sprouts	5 hrs	4–6 days	3–4 cups
4 Tbs	Fenugreek	2–15 hrs	1–3 days	1 cup
1 cup	Filberts	12–15 hrs		1¼ cups
1 cup	Garbanzo beans	12–48 hrs	2–4 days	3–4 cups
1 cup	Green lentils	24 hrs	1–3 days	2¾ cups
1 cup	Red lentils	8 hrs	1 day	2¾ cups
1 cup	Macadamia nuts	4–8 hrs	1 day	1¼ cups
1 cup	Mung beans	24–36 hrs	1–3 days	3¾ cups
1 Tbs	Onion seed	12 hrs	4–5 days	2 cups
1 cup	Peas	24–36 hrs	2–4 days	2½ cups
1 cup	Pecans	2–8 hrs	1 day	1⅛ cup

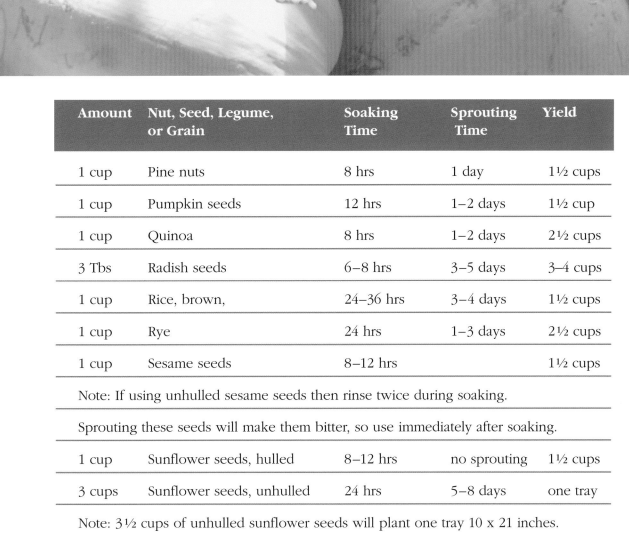

Amount	Nut, Seed, Legume, or Grain	Soaking Time	Sprouting Time	Yield
1 cup	Pine nuts	8 hrs	1 day	1½ cups
1 cup	Pumpkin seeds	12 hrs	1–2 days	1½ cup
1 cup	Quinoa	8 hrs	1–2 days	2½ cups
3 Tbs	Radish seeds	6–8 hrs	3–5 days	3–4 cups
1 cup	Rice, brown,	24–36 hrs	3–4 days	1½ cups
1 cup	Rye	24 hrs	1–3 days	2½ cups
1 cup	Sesame seeds	8–12 hrs		1½ cups

Note: If using unhulled sesame seeds then rinse twice during soaking.

Sprouting these seeds will make them bitter, so use immediately after soaking.

1 cup	Sunflower seeds, hulled	8–12 hrs	no sprouting	1½ cups
3 cups	Sunflower seeds, unhulled	24 hrs	5–8 days	one tray

Note: 3½ cups of unhulled sunflower seeds will plant one tray 10 x 21 inches.

1 cup	Walnuts, shelled	6–8 hrs	no sprouting	1⅛ cup
1 cup	Wild rice	4–36 hrs	3–6 days	3 cups
1 cup	Wheat, soft	24 hrs	1–3 days	1¾ cups
3 cups	Wheat, hard winter	24 hrs	6–8 days	one tray

Note: Hard winter wheat is the best for growing wheatgrass.

2½ cups–3 cups will yield approximately one tray of wheatgrass.

Cut in Chunks

Cut into pieces that will move easily through the juicer, food processor, or blender.

Coarsely Chopped

This results in pieces no larger than the end of your thumb. It can be a combination of small chunks and larger pieces.

Chopped

Smaller in size than "coarsely chopped," usually between 1 and 1/2 inch and roughly uniform in size.

Diced

Chopped into cubes approximately 1/3–1/2 inch in length/width.

Minced

This is the smallest chop, used mostly for garlic and onions, although I will sometimes mince fresh parsley, chives, or dill for optimum seasoning.

Slivered

Thin strips of zucchini, bell peppers, or carrots, for example, are cut into pieces 4–5 inches in length.

Julienned

Very similar to "slivered" but squared off at the ends.

Grated

This can be accomplished with a hand grater or machine, and one can have small grated bits or larger shredded bits.

Pitted

Remove pits or seeds in olives, plums, and apricots, etc.

Tear

This refers to lettuces or other green leafy vegetables that are torn into bite-size pieces with the hands.

Plan

Remember you usually need to plan ahead with raw-food preparation. Know what you need to soak or dehydrate or ferment, as these processes can sometimes take up to two days to complete.

Keep Handy

Keep some soaked seeds such as almonds and sunflower seeds available in the fridge for quick, easy-to-make recipes and simple snacking.

Remember Beauty

Try to make the presentation of the food beautiful. This whets the appetite and assists with digestion, because digestion starts in the brain. We see, sense, and smell the food, which in turn starts secretion of the digestive enzymes that will receive the food in the stomach.

Have Fun!

In raw foods there is such an abundance of different colors and textures to choose from. Use these in contrasting ways to make the presentation of your meals interesting. Garnishing your meals with edible flowers and herbs, using different-color fruits and veggies, dressings or sauces, all give food that special flair. Be creative and have fun.

Pay Attention

If you are doing a cleanse or have difficulty with digestion, pay attention to the food combining rules. Make the necessary changes in the recipes.

Taste It

When dehydrating anything and you are not sure how long it takes to fully dry, just taste your food. If it is to your liking then it's ready. Dehydrating times can vary according to the humidity and temperature in the area where you live.

Eat in Season

It's always best to buy fruits and veggies that are in season. These can be substituted in many of the recipes.

Be Creative

The recipes in this book are guidelines, not absolute rules, so be creative and make them your own by altering ingredients or seasonings.

Soak Dried Fruits

I didn't include dried fruits in the soaking chart, so if you choose to use these, they are best used after they have been soaked. The recipes will specify the times.

Get Fresh Produce

Try to use the freshest possible produce, as it will have the most flavor. Leftovers can be dehydrated, juiced, or frozen, whichever is most appropriate.

Adjust

In the recipes where you see measurements of 1–2 cups (or more than one measurement), always start with the lesser amount. You can add more if desired, but it's difficult if you add too much. I give a wide range of measurement in many of the recipes, since some people like more or less sweetness or spiciness; and sometimes vegetables have more juice (water) than at other times. Always taste your recipe, and then make your adjustment to your taste before serving.

Love

Prepare your food with lots of LOVE.

Tangerine Dream

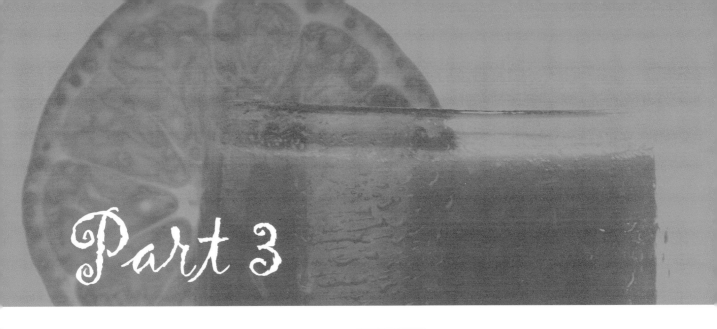

Part 3

Recipes
for Health
and Beauty

Juices

Juices are the living waters that are extracted from fruits and vegetables. They abound with enzymes, vitamins, minerals, and phytochemicals/nutrients. Juices are most efficiently made by putting these foods through the hopper of a juicer, which extracts the juice and spits out the pulp. Because juices are devoid of the plant's fiber, they are very concentrated in nutrients and can offer amazing healing benefits to the body. They tend to be very alkalizing and rejuvenating. I try to do a three-day juice cleanse at least once a month to give my body a break from digesting heavier foods and to release stored toxins. I also recommend supplementing your everyday diet with at least two freshly squeezed juices to supply nutrients that you may not be getting in your foods.

Fresh juices take only a few minutes to make. It is best to drink the fruit juices in the morning when the body is in a natural cleansing cycle, and the vegetable juices in the afternoon when the body is in a building cycle.

When making your juices remember to use fresh organic produce—preferably what is in season—and drink your juices within fifteen minutes of being made, as they will progressively lose their enzyme strength and nutrient value as they sit. This is a rule and not a law, as you'll see that I recommend many of the juice concoctions be chilled before drinking. I will sometimes add ice cubes and blend my juice if I'm in a hurry and can't refrigerate.

If you have any sugar sensitivity it is best to avoid the concentrated fruit juices, or to add equal parts of water to help dilute the sugar. In such cases I recommend more of the vegetable juices but go easy with the carrots and beets due to their high sugar content. If you need to sweeten a green juice you can add a piece of apple or pear, although this is not in alignment with the food combining rules. Experiment with yourself in this respect. If you have allergies or digestive problems, then stay with the rules of the stomach. If you don't experience any adverse symptoms, then be creative. It is best to peel oranges and grapefruits if putting through a juicer; otherwise use a citrus juicer.

Always peel waxed produce. When juicing apples it's best to remove the apple seeds, as they do contain a toxin.

For wonderful juice recipes that address specific health issues I invite you to read *Juicing for Life* by Cherie Calbom and Maureen Keane (see Recommended Reading list.) It addresses every disorder from A to Z.

Hawaiian Sunset

This juice is a great digestive aid and would work best served before a meal.

½ pineapple
¼ medium-size Mexican papaya
½–1 inch ginger (start with less)
½ cup cranberries or 2 tsp cranberry concentrate

Cut outer skin off pineapple and papaya and cut fruit into chunks that will easily move through your juicer hopper. Juice pineapple and ginger together and keep separate from juiced papaya. Pour into fancy glasses then add the juiced papaya and dribble with cranberry concentrate or juiced cranberries. Garnish juice with a slice of orange. Serves 2.

Pineapple Orange Zinger

½ pineapple
4 oranges
1 cup hibiscus sun tea

This recipe is loaded with lots of vitamin C and bromelain (anti-inflammatory enzyme). It's a great juice combination even without the tea.

Peel pineapple and juice. Remove orange skins and juice, or juice in citrus juicer.

Make hibiscus sun tea by putting 2 tsp hibiscus leaves in a pint of pure water and letting it sit in the sun 6–8 hours. Combine with the juices and garnish with a slice of lemon. Serves 2–4.

Berry Melon

¼ watermelon
½ cantaloupe
6 strawberries

This makes a great kidney cleanser and skin tonic. Strawberries contain natural pain inhibitors, and watermelon helps to flush the kidneys.

Peel watermelon and cantaloupe then juice together with fresh strawberries. Try this without the strawberries and add a little ginger for a nice variation. Serves 4.

Bloody Mary

4 apples, yellow or Red Delicious
½ beet
1 lime
½ inch ginger
Sprig of mint

Just what the liver needs and loves.

In the Champion juicer, juice apples, beet, lime, and ginger. I like to serve this cold with a sprig of mint for garnish. Serves 2.

Master Coco Cleanser

1 young coconut
1–2 limes or 1 lemon
⅛–¼ tsp cayenne, depending on its heat

This is a great cleansing juice that is full of minerals and enzymes, helps to break up mucus in the body, and strengthens the heart.

Open coconut with machete and drain water. Juice limes or lemons and add to water, along with cayenne pepper. Serves 1–2.

Rejuvelac

1 cup sprouted wheat berries or rye berries (see section on sprouting)

3 cups pure water

Additional water to make one gallon

Full of acidophilus, enzymes, and B vitamins.

Soak wheat berry or rye berry seeds for 12–24 hours, rinsing twice during that time. Sprout for two days until seed has a tail on it approximately ¼ inch. Place seeds in blender with 3 cups of water and blend for 15 seconds to help crack the seed. Transfer the mixture into a gallon container and fill with additional water. Leave on the kitchen counter for two days until fermented. Strain and refrigerate. Will last two weeks.

Note: If your rejuvelac goes off on you, it may be that the temperature in your home is too hot. Put in a cooler space.

Cranberry Cocktail

1 cup cranberries

6 apples, seeded

1 young coconut or rejuvelac

Twist of lime or lemon

Garnish with lime or lemon

Wonderful for any bladder disorders.

Juice cranberries and apples and add to coconut water from a fresh young coconut.

You can try this one without the coco water as a variation. Serves 2–4.

Apple Mint Fizz

6–8 sprigs fresh mint

4 green apples, seeded

1 lime

1 cup rejuvelac

Mint for garnish

This drink is very refreshing, with lots of those friendly bacteria that the intestines need.

Juice mint, apples, and lime together and serve in nice cold glasses or with ice. Add rejuvelac to taste and garnish with mint. Serves 2.

Wendy Bird Special

2 cups fresh-squeezed orange juice
or grapefruit juice
½ cup fresh aloe vera
1–2 Tbs flax oil
1 clove garlic
½–1 tsp minced ginger
Dash of cayenne

This drink is a powerful liver and bowel detoxifier and immune booster, and very healing to all skin conditions.

Fillet the fresh aloe vera plant and place in the blender with all other ingredients. Blend well. Serves 2.

Cantaloupe Cream

½ cantaloupe
½ inch ginger
(optional)
Mint for garnish

This recipe provides a very good source of bioflavonoids and is great for your skin.

Peel cantaloupe unless it's organic, and juice with its seeds and ginger. Serve cold and garnish with mint. Serves 1–2.

Kiwi Punch

4 apples
2 pears
6 kiwis
½ inch ginger

Melt the fat away with this one.

Juice all ingredients. Serves 1–2.

Peaches 'n' Cream

6 peaches
2 pears
1 apple
1 cup water or coconut water
2 bananas

Rich in enzymes and nutrients, this drink leaves you feeling peachy cream.

Juice peaches, pears, and apple and blend in banana. Serves 1–2.

Cantaloupe Cream

Hibiscus Cooler

2 quarts pure water
½ cup hibiscus flowers
½ cup chopped fresh mint leaves
1 pint fresh-squeezed orange,
pineapple, tangelo, or tangerine juice
or combination
Honey, agave syrup,
or stevia to sweeten
Garnish: Slices of orange twist,
pineapple spears, or frozen red grapes

Hibiscus flowers are very popular in Mexico, and that's where that I learned to make this. Hibiscus flowers are abundant in vitamin C and help to strengthen the immune system.

Place hibiscus flowers in water and set in the sun to make a sun tea. Add the fresh-squeezed juices and sweeten to your taste. Garnish and serve chilled. Makes 2½ quarts.

Tequila Sunrise

4 oranges
1 pomegranate
1 lime
¼ tsp jalapeño
Sprig of mint for garnish

A little spicy but yummy!

Juice oranges, then blend with pomegranate, lime, and jalapeño. Strain and serve chilled with a sprig of mint. Serves 1–2.

Tangerine Dream

6 tangerines
1 cup of red grapes
1 grapefruit
½ lemon

This vitamin C booster is a great way to start your day.

Juice all ingredients. Serves 2.

Ginger Berry Cocktail

1 quart blueberries
1 inch ginger
4 cups green or purple grapes
1 lime
Water (optional)

This combination is a great anti-aging formula and skin tonic.

Juice all ingredients and serve chilled. Add water if too concentrated. Serves 2.

Fruity Tea

3 oranges
3 apples, seeded
1 lime
2 cinnamon sticks
1 small piece of ginger
2 quarts pure water

Can be enjoyed warm or cold.

Juice oranges, apples, and lime and add to water. Place in a pan with cinnamon sticks and heat on very low heat for 15 minutes, not to exceed 105 degrees.

Cherry Mango Cocktail

4 cups cherries, pitted
2 cups strawberries
1 mango
1 coconut

Out with the gout! This is a great remedy for any build-up of uric acid in the body.

Open coconut and extract the water. Place in your blender with all other ingredients and enjoy this delicious smoothie.

Beety Mango

¼ cup beet juice
1½ cups rejuvelac, coco water, or apple juice
1 lime
1 large ripe mango
Lime twist for garnish

This one is so delicious and presents well with a twist of lime.

Juice beet and lime and add to blender with rejuvelac, mango, and a little ice to chill. Blend well and serve in tall fancy glasses with a twist of lime. Serves 2.

Applecot-Grape Ambrosia

2 apples
4 apricots
1 pound of grapes
1 lemon peeled
Water (optional)

Tasty!

Juice all ingredients. Garnish with a twist of orange. If too concentrated add a little water to taste.

Beety Mango

Horchata

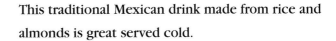

2 cups sprouting brown rice

*3 cups pure water
or young coconut water*

*1¼ cups soaked
and blanched almonds*

2 tsp cinnamon

*¼ tsp lime zest
or grate the skin from 1 lime*

¼ cup honey

Additional water to taste

This traditional Mexican drink made from rice and almonds is great served cold.

Soak rice overnight; rinse and drain. Add rice, water or coconut water, almonds, cinnamon, honey, and lime zest to the Vita-Mix and blend well, adding more water if necessary. Strain mixture and serve cold with a twist of lime.

Smoothies

Smoothies feature all the benefits of juicing with the addition of the fiber from the fruits. Smoothies are best made in a Vita-Mix or blender. I have known people to use a food processor, but in my opinion it does not get the mixture smooth enough. If I want to serve a smoothie chilled I will add some ice cubes or use frozen fruit, cut into pieces that will easily go through the juice hopper. Basic combinations for smoothies are suggested below. Play with the amounts yourself and be creative. In the winter months I will sometimes augment with ginger or jalapeño to add some heat to my digestive fire.

Start with some kind of liquid base such as purified water, coco water, fresh-squeezed juice, rejuvelac, or any of the nut and seed milks. Simply add your fruit fresh or frozen and blend well. If you have sugar-related problems, use half juice and half water. Sometimes I will put a tablespoon or two of flax oil or avocado into my smoothie to help slow down the release of sugar into the bloodstream. It's a great way to get those essential fatty acids.

Following are some wonderful combinations for smoothies. If you are missing a fruit then substitute another. Be creative and enjoy.

Note: I will often add supplements to my smoothies such as Nature's First Food (powdered green super-foods), Vitamin C crystals, MSM (organic sulfur), bee pollen, maca, goji berries, tocotrienols, coconut butter or oil, cacao nibs or powder, hemp seeds, the flax oils and even some herbal tinctures. (See the appendix for more information about some of these supplements.) I like to do this in the morning for my breakfast, as it really gives a nutritious, easily absorbed energy boost.

I have not included quantities here but 1 cup of juice with a little of each fruit will serve 2 people. These smoothies will last about two days, but try to drink them after they have been freshly made for maximum enzymes and flavor.

Combine the following as a start to your smoothie creations.

- Apples, banana, papaya. Juice the apples then blend with banana and papaya.

- Oranges, kiwi, banana. Juice the oranges and blend with kiwi and banana.

- Pineapple, papaya, mango. Juice pineapple and blend papaya and mango.

- Pineapple. banana, apricots. Juice pineapple and blend banana and apricots.

- Apples, peaches, banana. Juice apples and blend with peaches and banana.

- Pineapple, blueberries, banana. Juice pineapple and blend with blueberries and banana.

- Oranges, apples, strawberries. Juice oranges and blend with apples and strawberries.

- Oranges, peaches, pears, plums. Juice oranges and blend the rest.

- Pineapple, papaya, banana, persimmons. Juice pineapple and blend in the rest.

- Pineapple, banana, strawberry, raspberry, boysenberry. Juice pineapple and blend the rest.

Green Drinks

Wheatgrass Juice Cocktail

Red winter wheat, sprouted and grown for approximately 12–14 days. See section on sprouting, especially the sprouting chart.

Cut wheatgrass approximately 1 inch above the ground. Wash, rinse, and drain. Feed wheatgrass slowly into wheatgrass juicer. (For equipment models, see the Resources list.) Drink immediately after processing. Wait at least an hour before eating a meal or at least two hours after eating a meal.

Juice combinations for vegetables are as varied as the fruit combinations for fruit juices. You can use any combination but remember that parsley, garlic, onion, spinach, beet greens, dandelion, wild weeds, and kale can be very strong-tasting greens (bitter). These stronger juices are extremely beneficial and have wonderful healing properties. (See *Juicing for Life.*) But for ease of regular consumption I recommend combining them with milder juices such as cucumber or celery. Try to use the freshest produce for the best results.

For a vegetable juice base, use carrot, cucumber, celery, or any combination of these. To that base you can add parsley, spinach, red bell pepper, cabbage, beets, leeks, radish, squash, tomatoes, watercress, zucchini, lettuce, buckwheat greens, sunflower greens, Swiss chard, arugula and/or beet greens.

To prepare, simply wash and cut into hopper-size pieces then juice. I like to add ginger and garlic to my veggie juices at times, especially if it's cold outside, for that additional heat that it creates internally.

Sprouted Green Juice

Juices or smoothies can have living green sprouts added to them. I prefer the buckwheat and sunflower greens, but you can choose from alfalfa, broccoli, or clover as well. Simply put a handful into the blender with a cup or two of juice for flavor.

1–2 cups juice (carrot, tomato, apple, pineapple, or carrot/celery)
1 handful of sprouts
Squeeze of lemon or lime

Blend and garnish with mango.

Alkalizing Blend

This recipe will quickly assist the body in neutralizing acids.

1 cucumber
4–6 stalks of celery
4–6 leaves of kale
Handful of arugula

Wash and peel cucumber if waxed, and cut celery into 2-inch chunks so that the celery strings do not tie up the juicer. Juice all ingredients and drink immediately. You can make this a milder-tasting juice by adding more cucumber or celery. Serves 2.

Nut & Seed
Milks & Shakes

These "milks" are made from soaked nuts and seeds and then blended with water. They make a wonderful substitute for dairy milks and are superior in nutrients and enzymes. They can be easily sweetened and flavored with honey, agave syrup, stevia, dates, raisins, vanilla, or cinnamon.

The best-tasting and most nutritious of the milks are those made from almonds and sesame seeds or a combination of those. You can also make milks from sunflower seeds, walnuts, cashews, pecans, filberts, or pumpkin seeds. These milks can be used as bases in smoothies, soups, dressings, sauces, yogurts, and ice creams.

They provide high levels of protein, fat, and calcium along with additional calories, so if you are wanting to gain weight or build muscles then eating these foods will help. I recommend a wonderful book called *Raw Power* by Steve Arlin for anyone who is doubtful about being a body builder on raw foods. (See Recommended Reading list.) I have personally met the author and he is built like a gorilla and eats 100 percent raw food.

To make the nut and seed milks, start by soaking your seeds. Refer to the soaking and sprouting chart in the more detailed section on Sprouting, above. You'll want to keep a copy of this chart handy until you get the knack of soaking times. (It won't take long!)

Blend the soaked seeds or nuts with purified water and strain through a fine sieve, seed bag, or cheesecloth. If using almonds you may want to blanch and peel the skins for easier digestion. This is time-consuming but not mandatory. As always, plan ahead.

Sesame Milk

1 cup soaked sesame seeds
2–3 cups water

Rinse seeds, blend and strain. This is delicious over cereals or enjoyed by itself as milk.

Note: To sweeten, blend with dates, agave syrup, honey, or stevia.

Sunflower Milk

1 cup soaked sunflower seeds
2–3 cups water

Rinse seeds, blend and strain. Save pulp for other uses or discard. Sweeten with honey, agave syrup, or stevia, or blend with dates.

Almond Milk

1 cup almonds
4–6 cups pure water

Soak almonds 10–12 hours. Rinse well. If you want a clean white milk then blanch almonds to remove skins. Blend with water and strain. If you want thicker milk add less water; for thinner milk, add more water. See what works for you and your taste. Milks can be sweetened with honey, agave syrup, stevia, or dates.

Nut & Seed Shakes

These are heavier smoothies or shakes and not recommended if you have to adhere to the Rules of the Stomach. They consist of a combination of fruits, nuts, and seeds and/or their milks.

Almond Date Shake

2 cups almond milk
2 frozen bananas
6–8 dates, soaked 30 minutes
Dash of vanilla or cinnamon (optional)

Place dates in a bowl with just enough water to cover. Let sit for 30 minutes, then drain. Blend dates, nut milk, banana, and flavoring. Serve immediately. Serves 2.

Chocolate Almond Date Shake

Umm, yummy! Follow recipe for Almond Date Shake and blend in additional 3–4 Tbs cacao powder (or carob powder).

Coconut Almond Shake

1 young coconut
½ cup almonds
4 soaked Medjool dates
2 Tbs agave syrup or honey (optional)
1 tsp vanilla
Dash of cinnamon

One of my favorites and full of protein, calcium, and the good kind of fat.

Cut open coconut and pour water into Vita-Mix or blender. Remove coconut meat and blend with coconut water, soaked dates, almonds, vanilla, agave syrup, and cinnamon.

Note: This recipe may be sweet enough without the added agave syrup, so try it first without the syrup. You can always add it later. Make sure that the coconuts are young to medium so that the coconut meat is soft and rubbery, not hard.

Bugs Bunny Shake

Lots of vitamin A, and the good kind of fat that the body needs. Great drink for healthy skin.

1 mature coconut to make coconut cream
1 pound of carrots

Open coconut and save water for another recipe. With a butter knife carefully remove the hard white coconut meat inside the shell. Juice the coconut meat through a Champion juicer. Juice carrots and add to the coconut cream. Shake and enjoy! Serves 2.

Apple Banana Zinc Shake

This drink provides wonderful support for the prostate gland and urinary system, along with enhancing the immune system in general and supplying lots of vitamins and minerals.

4 apples
2 bananas
2 tsp of cranberry concentrate or juice from ½ cup fresh cranberries
¼–½ cup soaked pumpkin seeds
1 lime or ½ lemon

Juice apples, cranberries, and lime or lemon. Add to blender and blend with banana and pumpkin seeds until smooth and creamy. Serves 2–4.

RECIPES FOR HEALTH AND BEAUTY

Bugs Bunny Shake

Creamy Corn Chowder

Soups

In making any soup (or sauce or salad dressing), it is best to think of its three components. The first is some kind of liquid base; the second is a vegetable or fruit; and the third is a thickener. You may make a soup, sauce, or dressing that does not need a thickener because the vegetables or fruits supply sufficient texture. With this three-part guideline, experiment and create your own special soups.

Choose one or more from each category:

Liquid Base

Pure Water

Rejuvelac

Coconut Water

Fresh-Squeezed Juices

Nut and/or Seed Milks

Vegetable / Fruit

Main Vegetable or Fruit

Additional Vegetables or Fruits

Herbs, Spices, and other Flavorings

Seaweeds (such as Dulse and Kelp)

Thickener

Avocado

Seed Cheese

Nuts and Seeds

Flax Meal

Once you learn this triple formula, you can develop your own recipes. Unless your main ingredient is tomatoes or cucumbers, which are very juicy, you will need some kind of liquid base. Avocado as a thickener will give your recipe that desirable creamy-smooth texture, while flax meal will give it a more nutty texture and taste.

To make flax meal: Grind flax seeds in a small coffee or spice grinder. I like to soak and dehydrate my flax seeds first to get the added nutrients. When using flax meal as a thickener, remember that the longer the recipe stands, the thicker it will get, so start with a small quantity first. You can always add more later if you want your soup, sauce, or dressing to be thicker.

These recipes are somewhat interchangeable, and it's possible to use a leftover blended soup as a dressing or sauce. These are best used within two days, as enzymes and nutrients will be lost after that. The following recipes are made up of the three components: liquid base, vegetable(s) or fruit(s), and a thickener. Note that items printed with capital letters, such as Tomato Powder, indicate a recipe found in this book—see appropriate sections.

Sopa de Luis

Tomato Basil Soup

1 small to medium onion

12 stalks of celery

4 carrots

½–1 jicama (enough to make
1 cup of juice)

8–10 tomatoes (enough to make
5 cups of juice and pulp)

2 cloves garlic

5 cups tomato pulp
(from making the juice)

1 Tbs Tomato Powder
(see Seasoning Powders)

½ cup chopped basil

2 Tbs dulse or 1 tsp Celtic sea salt

6 basil springs for garnish

This light soup would complement any Italian entrée. It is rich with the mixed flavors of tomato and basil.

Juice the first six ingredients. When you juice the tomatoes, reserve the tomato pulp (about 5 cups) to add back to the soup for texture. Transfer the juices to a blender along with the tomato pulp, Tomato Powder, and dulse or sea salt. Blend to a smooth consistency then add the chopped basil. Blend just enough to mix in the basil. You do not want to pulverize the basil, as this will turn the soup brown. Garnish each bowl with a sprig of fresh basil. Serves 6.

Note: Leftover Tomato Basil Soup, blended with enough avocado to make a smoothie-type consistency and then dehydrated, makes an excellent vegetable wrap or burrito skin. See Tortillas (in Wraps section).

Sopa de Luis

Juice the following:

2 large carrots

4 tomatoes

8 stalks celery

½ onion

Blend in the following:

1–2 tomatoes

1 cucumber

½ avocado

¼ cup basil

2 cloves garlic

1 tsp dulse

½ tsp Celtic sea salt

¼ tsp habanero chile
or dried cayenne pepper

2 basil springs for garnish

This is a heavier-bodied soup combining the flavors of Italian dishes. The juices combined with the rest of the vegetables provide all the nutrients your body needs.

Add juiced ingredients to Vita-Mix or blender. Add the remaining ingredients and blend until smooth. Garnish each bowl with a sprig of basil. Serves 2.

Curried Carrot Soup

Cucumber Cilantro Soup

1 Tbs yellow miso mixed in ½ cup water

1 lemon or lime, juiced

1 cucumber

2 tomatoes

¼ cup cilantro

1 clove garlic

¼ tsp jalapeño

1 tsp ginger

To garnish, mix the following:

1 diced tomato

⅓ cup diced cucumber

½ cup cubed avocado

¼ cup minced cilantro with a squeeze of lime juice

Blend vegetable ingredients with miso and lime juice. Then add chopped garnish on top. Drizzle top with 1 Tbs Flavored Olive Oil (see Marinades and Dressings). Serves 2.

Curried Carrot Soup

Juice the following:

Approximately 6 carrots to make 1 cup juice

1 cup orange squash to make ½ cup squash juice

¼ cup apple juice

¼ onion, juiced

2 ears corn, reserve half for garnish

¼ avocado

2 Tbs pumpkin seeds, ground, or 1 Tbs pumpkin seed butter (optional)

½ tsp dried basil

1 clove garlic

¼–½ tsp curry

Dash of Celtic sea salt to taste

½ cup grated carrot for garnish

Blend juices with remainder of ingredients. Add reserved corn and grated carrot for texture. Warm in the dehydrator. Serves 2.

Variation: Carrot Ginger Soup

Follow the recipe for the Curried Carrot Soup, but instead of using curry for spicing, add a 1-inch piece of ginger to be juiced with the carrots, squash, apple, and onion.

Note: This is a great soup for those cold winter days, as the ginger will quickly warm the body.

Juice enough of the following ingredients to make:

1 cup carrot juice

1 cup beet juice

¼ cup apple juice

2 cups orange juice

1 lemon, juiced

Filling:

1 beet, grated

1 carrot, grated

1 cup purple cabbage, shredded

¼ cup chopped green onion

¼ cup fresh dill, finely chopped

1 tsp minced jalapeño

2–3 cloves garlic

2 tsp ginger

1 tsp Celtic sea salt

Garnish:

1 avocado chopped and
1 apple shredded

Put juices in the blender after making them and blend with your garlic, ginger, jalapeño, and sea salt. Pour into individual bowls and stir in equal amounts of grated beets, carrots, cabbage, and dill. Garnish with chopped avocado, apples, and a sprinkle of dill. Serves 4–6.

78

Asparagus Soup

½–1 avocado

1 cup chopped asparagus, reserve tips for garnish

1–2 stalks chopped celery

1 cup spinach

2 cups water

1 green onion, chopped

2 Tbs mixed fresh herbs (thyme, tarragon, rosemary)

2 cloves garlic

Bragg's Liquid Aminos, Nama Shoyu, or Celtic sea salt to taste

Dash of cayenne pepper

Radishes for garnish

Combine all ingredients in the blender and blend until creamy and smooth. Strain through a sieve to remove any coarse fiber. Serve in soup bowls, swirling in a little olive oil on the top of each. Garnish with asparagus tips and shaved radishes. Serves 2–3.

Creamy Corn Chowder

3 cups almond milk

3 cups corn cut from the cob, reserve 1 cup

½ avocado

2 green onions

2 lemons, juiced

½ tsp cumin

1 tsp fresh ginger

¼–½ tsp jalapeño

2–3 cloves garlic

½ tsp Celtic sea salt or dash of Nama Shoyu

Blend in the Vita-Mix all ingredients except the reserved corn. Stir in corn kernels and sprinkle with a little cumin and dulse flakes. Serves 4.

Energy Soup

2 cups carrot juice

1 cup cucumber juice

4 cups buckwheat greens

2 cups sunflower greens

1 avocado

½ onion

2–3 cloves garlic

1 tsp minced ginger

2 tsp kelp, dulse,
or Celtic sea salt to taste

This quick blended soup is made from a combination of fresh-squeezed juices, sprouted greens, spices, and a thickener. Using different juices or combinations of juices and vegetables can provide plenty of variety. For the thickener I would stay with either a little avocado or some ground-up flax seed.

Blend all together in the Vita-Mix and eat immediately for optimum benefits. Serves 3.

Creamy Cilantro Spinach Soup

1 cup carrot juice

1½ cups tomato juice

2 large handfuls spinach,
approximately 4 cups

1 handful cilantro,
approximately 1 cup

½ avocado

2 cloves garlic

½ tsp minced ginger

4 green onions

Dash of Celtic sea salt to taste

Dash of cayenne
or minced jalapeño to taste

Garnish: Cashew Cream
(see Yogurt, Creams, and Cheeses)

Blend juices with other ingredients. Add a little water if too thick. Blend until smooth and serve warm or chilled. Garnish with Cashew Cream. Serves 3–4.

Coconut Thai Soup

2 cups coconut water
½ cup cashew butter
1 cucumber, peeled
1–2 tsp ginger
3 cloves garlic
2 lemons
2 tsp galanga
¼ cup (about 2–3 Tbs) chopped lemon grass
1 cup long string mushrooms
1 cup chopped tomatoes
½ cup chopped mint leaves
¼ cup chopped cilantro
¼ cup chopped basil
1 Tbs coconut oil (optional)

Add coconut water to blender or Vita-Mix and blend with cucumber, cashew butter, ginger, garlic, lemon juice, galanga, and lemon grass. Blend until smooth. Add the remaining ingredients. Drizzle a little coconut oil over each bowl. Serves 4.

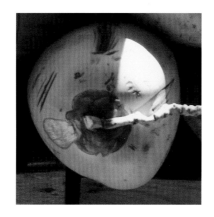

Gazpacho

4 cups diced tomatoes
2 cups diced cucumber
1 cup minced red bell pepper
1 cup diced papaya
1½ cup minced cilantro
1–2 lemons, juiced
½ tsp Celtic sea salt or dash of Nama Shoyu
1¼ tsp minced jalapeño
1–2 cloves garlic, minced

Mix all ingredients together and serve in soup bowls. Drizzle a little olive oil over each. If you want more of a liquid base, then blend a little of the mixture in the blender and add back to the rest of the ingredients. Serve chilled. Serves 4.

Carrot Squash Bisque

1 cup almond milk

1 cup carrot juice

½ cup squash juice

1 peeled carrot, chopped into chunks

½ cup chopped squash

1 avocado

*½ cup corn cut from the cob,
reserve half for garnish*

1–2 green onions, minced

2 cloves garlic

½ tsp cumin

¼ tsp nutmeg

½ tsp Celtic sea salt or dash of Nama Shoyu

Add almond milk and juices to the blender and blend in all ingredients except ¼ cup of corn and minced green onion. Blend until smooth then garnish with corn kernels and minced green onions. Serves 3–4.

Minestrone

This thick hearty soup has a full-bodied flavor and is a meal in itself.

1 cup carrot juice

1 cup tomato juice

1/2 cup thick almond milk

*2 tsp Tomato Powder (see Seasoning Powders),
or 3 sun-dried tomatoes, soaked*

1/4 cup thinly sliced yellow string beans

1/4 cup thinly sliced purple string beans (optional)

1/4 cup fresh peas from the pod

1/4 cup fresh corn cut from the cob

2 green onions, minced

1/4 cup chopped red bell peppers

1/2 cup diced tomatoes

1/4 cup diced yellow zucchini

1 tsp fresh oregano

1 Tbs fresh minced parsley

1/2 tsp fresh thyme

1 tsp Celtic sea salt

1/8 tsp crushed black peppercorns

2–3 cloves garlic

Flavored Olive Oil (see Marinades and Dressings)

Blend juices, almond milk, and Tomato Powder with seasonings until a smooth consistency is achieved, then add all the other ingredients. Garnish with a dribble of Flavored Olive Oil. Serve immediately. Serves 3–4.

Mushroom Almondine Soup

2 cups pure water
or young coconut water
1 cup almonds, soaked overnight
3 cups mushrooms, halved
(crimini or shiitake)
2 green onions
(reserve 1 onion for garnish)
1 Tbs olive oil
Dash of Celtic sea salt
¼ cup chopped mushrooms

This soup makes a wonderful gravy or sauce. It is rich in flavor as is, or you can add a little flax meal for a nuttier flavor. Just be aware that flax meal will thicken very rapidly and you may need to add more liquid. In the blender combine water, almonds, onion, mushrooms, salt, and olive oil. Blend until creamy and smooth. Garnish with chopped mushrooms and minced green onions.

Swiss Chard & Mung Bean Soup

½ bunch Swiss chard or mixture of
Swiss chard and kale, chopped
1 Tbs olive oil
½ tsp minced garlic
4–6 cups Miso Broth (see below)
1 cup mung bean sprouts
2 green onions, minced
1 tsp Celtic sea salt, Nama Shoyu,
or Bragg's to taste
¼ tsp minced jalapeño or cayenne
Squash blossoms

This soup is full of vitamins and enzymes. It can be served warm by slowly heating the broth then adding the greens and sprouts. If you do this make sure not to heat above 105 degrees.

Boil some water and let sit for a few minutes to cool off. Very quickly pour water over Swiss chard or kale to lightly wilt greens. It is best to do this in a strainer over the sink. Blend miso broth with olive oil, garlic, salt, and jalapeño in blender. Pour into a large soup bowl or serving tureen and add greens, onions, and sprouts. Garnish with squash blossoms. Serves 4–6.

Miso Broth

Yellow miso

To make miso broth, simply add 1–2 Tbs miso to 1 cup water. To make 4–6 cups of broth, add 4–6 Tbs miso. I prefer to blend the miso in a little water and then add it back to the liquid. This way you eliminate the lumps.

Balinese Soup

2 cups tomato juice (save pulp)
½ cup orange juice
⅓ cup sweet onion, chopped
1–2 cloves garlic
1 tsp curry powder
1 Tbs Tamarind Puree,*
dissolved in ¼ cup hot water
(see Sauces and Dips)
2 Tbs olive oil
1 tsp orange zest
Honey to taste

This soup has all the flavors of Bali. It is one of the trickier soups to make, and some adjustments may be necessary to get the right taste. However, if you do, this soup will satisfy all those desires for Indonesian flavors.

Juice tomatoes and place both juice and pulp in the Vita-Mix. Add all the other ingredients and blend really well. Add honey to taste. Serves 2.

*Note: If you're in a hurry, you can substitute the Tamarind Purée with tamarind paste available in Asian grocery stores.

Mango Cucumber Soup

4 ripe mangos
(reserve one mango for garnish)
2 large cucumbers
¼ cup fresh orange juice
3 Tbs lemon or lime juice
2 Tbs olive oil
2 Tbs chili powder
¼ tsp Celtic sea salt
Dash of cayenne or jalapeño
Garnish: Tomatillo Bits
(see Seasoning Powders)

Wash and peel mangos and cucumbers, reserving one mango for garnish. Cut in chunks and put in the blender with other ingredients. Blend until smooth. Chop remaining mango and add to soup. Sprinkle dried Tomatillo Bits on top of each soup bowl.

Carrot Flax Seed Soup

2 cups carrot juice

2–3 Tbs flax meal

1 tsp ginger

1 garlic clove

1/4 tsp cayenne

1 tsp dulse

1/2–1 tsp Mexican Seasoning Mix
(see Seasoning Powders)

2 Tbs lemon juice

Dash of Bragg's
or Celtic sea salt to taste

2 Tbs olive oil

2 Tbs macadamia nut butter

8–10 soaked almonds

This soup has a bit of a bite to it, so if you like spicy this one is for you. It is full of the essential fatty acids that flax seeds provide, along with lots of vitamin A.

Place all ingredients into blender and blend until smooth. Garnish with some grated carrot and chopped sunflower greens. Serve immediately. Serves 2.

Coconut Cilantro Lemongrass Soup

2 cups almond milk (make with
blanched almonds)

2 cups coconut water

1/2 cup Coconut Cream
(see Yogurt, Creams, and Cheeses)

2 cups young coconut meat

4 Tbs minced lemongrass

1 tsp minced ginger

1–2 cloves garlic

1 cup cilantro, chopped

1/2–1 tsp Celtic sea salt

Pinch of cayenne to taste

Coconut oil

This soup has a full-bodied taste and creamy texture, with the blended flavors of both coconut and almonds. The cilantro in this soup tops it off with yet another great flavor, making this one of the best raw cream soups I know of. This soup provides lots of protein and the best fat there is. Check out *The Miracles of Coconut Oil* (see Recommended Reading list).

Blend almond milk, coconut water, Coconut Cream, coconut meat, lemongrass, ginger, garlic, salt, and cayenne together. Add in cilantro last. Pour into individual bowls and drizzle a little coconut oil on top. Serves 4–6.

Cucumber Tahini Soup

2 cups cucumber juice
3 Tbs tahini
1½ cups diced cucumber
1 tsp dried dill
or 2 Tbs fresh dill, minced
½ tsp Celtic sea salt
1 clove garlic
½ tsp minced ginger
3 Tbs lemon or lime juice
Pinch of cayenne (optional)
Olive oil and fresh dill bits
for garnish

This creamy soup is both refreshing and nourishing. The kidneys love cucumbers; and tahini is one of the better sources of calcium and protein.

Juice cucumbers and put in the Vita-Mix with tahini, salt, garlic, dill, ginger, lemon juice, and cayenne. Blend well and add to serving bowls. Add in the cucumber, then drizzle the top with a little olive oil and fresh dill. Serve immediately. Serves 2.

Salads

Quinoa Pistachio Salad

1 cup quinoa, sprouted
(see section on sprouting)

½ peeled cucumber

½ red bell pepper, minced

½ cup diced red or yellow tomato

1 stalk celery, minced

2 green onions, minced

¼ cup parsley, minced

¼ cup pistachios

¼ cup raisins, soaked 1 hour

1 clove garlic, minced

¼ tsp minced ginger

1 lemon, juiced

2 Tbs olive oil

Dash of Celtic sea salt,
Nama Shoyu, or Bragg's

Mix all ingredients together and chill. Serves 2.

Vegetable Combo Medley

1 cup broccoli flowerets

1 cup cauliflower,
cut into bite-size pieces

1 medium carrot, sliced thin

1 yellow zucchini, sliced julienne

¼ cup red onion, sliced julienne

1 recipe Simple Marinade

Marinate the vegetables for 6 hours. Serve on a bed of butter lettuce and sprinkle with Gomasio (optional). Serves 4.

Eastern Exotic Carrot Salad

1 pound carrots, grated
2 Tbs olive oil
1 Tbs lemon juice
1 Tbs raw apple cider vinegar
or lemon juice
1 Tbs cold-pressed raw sesame oil
1–2 tsp white miso
1–2 tsp Nama Shoyu or Bragg's
1/4 cup thinly sliced onions
2 Tbs minced parsley
1/4 tsp minced fresh tarragon

Mix all ingredients together and serve chilled on a bed of butter lettuce. Serves 3–4.

89

Avocado Citrus Salad

1 pink grapefruit
1 white grapefruit
1 orange
2 avocados
3 Tbs olive oil
3 Tbs lemon juice
1 pound mixed baby greens
1 cup sunflower sprouts
1/2 tsp Celtic sea salt
Dash of cayenne
1/3 cup Almond Croutons (see section
on Croutons, Bread, etc.)
1/3 cup thinly sliced green onions

Peel skin and white membranes from the citrus fruit, and with a sharp knife carefully slice fruit from between inner membranes. Do this over a bowl that will catch any juice. Set aside the fruit segments. In a larger bowl mix salad greens and sprouts with the oil, lemon juice, citrus juice, and seasonings. Divide into six servings and top with avocado slices, citrus segments, chopped Almond Croutons, and green onions. Serves 6.

Wild Rice Salad

*2 cups wild rice, soaked for four days
(change water 2 times a day)*

1 cup diced cucumber

½ cup diced red bell pepper

½ cup minced celery

¼ cup chopped scallions

*½ cup mixed fresh herbs, chopped
(dill, basil, parsley)*

2 cloves minced garlic

¼ tsp minced ginger

2 Tbs lemon juice

*½–1 tsp Celtic sea salt,
Nama Shoyu, or Bragg's*

Dash of cayenne (optional)

2–3 Tbs olive oil

This salad makes a great stuffing for the Stuffed Cabbage Rolls (see Entrées) or Stuffed Cabbage Boats (see Side Dishes).

Soak rice until soft and chewy. Strain and mix in the remaining ingredients. Serve chilled. Serves 4.

Greek Salad with Feta Cheese

2 handfuls baby spinach

½ cup red onion, chopped

*¼ cup pine nuts,
soaked and dehydrated*

*¼ cup sun-dried black olives, pitted
(from Rawfood.com)*

1 handful small cherry tomatoes

*1 recipe Feta Cheese (see Yogurt,
Creams, and Cheeses)*

3 Tbs olive oil

1 Tbs lemon juice

1 clove garlic, minced

Dash of Celtic sea salt and black pepper

*Garnish with Gomasio
(see Seasoning Powders)*

In a bowl, toss the spinach with ¼ cup red onion, pine nuts, tomatoes, and olives, along with olive oil, lemon juice, garlic, sea salt, and black pepper. Sprinkle Feta Cheese on top and serve with Gomasio. Serves 2.

Green Papaya Salad

1½ cups green papaya, shredded

½ cup shredded carrot

½ cup shredded green cabbage

⅓ red onion, julienned

Mix all ingredients and set aside. Mix in dressing (see below). Toss just enough dressing into salad ingredients to moisten. Serve chilled with "Peanut" Sauce (see Sauces and Dips). Serves 2.

Green Papaya Dressing

¼ cup apple cider vinegar

⅓ cup raw sesame oil

¼ cup honey

3 Tbs Nama Shoyu

1–2 cloves garlic

1 Tbs minced galangal root

Thai chile pepper to taste

Blend all ingredients in the Vita-Mix.

Summer Coleslaw

¼ green cabbage, shredded

¼ purple cabbage, shredded

2 carrots, grated

1 yellow zucchini, grated

¼ cup minced red onion

½ cup fresh dill, chopped

1 tsp caraway seed, ground fine

1 recipe Mayonnaise
(see Sauces and Dips)

Combine all ingredients and serve chilled. Serves 4.

Rainbow Slaw

½ cup shredded carrot

½ cup shredded beet

½ cup shredded jicama

½ cup shredded zucchini

2 garlic cloves, grated fine

½ tsp grated ginger

¼ cup flax or olive oil

2 Tbs lemon or lime juice

1 Tbs Bragg's or Nama Shoyu

½ tsp dried dill

Fresh arugula or romaine lettuce

This rainbow mixture of root vegetables offers lots of fiber and roughage, combined with the delicate flavors of ginger and dill.

Mix all ingredients together and let marinate for 15 minutes. Serve on a bed of fresh arugula or romaine lettuce. Serves 2.

Arugula Walnut Blackberry Salad

2 cups young fresh arugula

1 cup mixed baby greens

¼ red onion, sliced thin

1 Tbs minced garlic chives (optional)

¼ cup fresh blackberries

¼ cup chopped walnuts

Blackberry Vinaigrette (see Strawberry Vinaigrette, in Marinades and Dressings section)

This salad is packed with nutrients and has a unique peppery taste. Try this with other berries for variety.

Wash and spin-dry greens. In a bowl mix onions, chives, and walnuts. Divide into servings and garnish with the fresh berries. Add berries last so tossing them with the greens does not break them up. Serve with Blackberry Vinaigrette. Serves 2.

Arugula Broccoli Salad

⅓ cup diced red onions

1½ cups chopped fresh organic broccoli flowerets

4 cups arugula

⅓ cup corn kernels

¼ jicama, julienned (optional)

½ cup sesame oil and olive oil mixed

¼ cup water

3 Tbs lemon or lime juice

2 cloves garlic, minced

Bragg's or Celtic sea salt to taste

Dash of cayenne

Chopped walnuts for garnish

This salad has a peppery taste mixed with an Asian flavor and is full of calcium and B vitamins.

Combine oil, lemon juice, water, garlic, Bragg's, and cayenne. Marinate onions, corn, and chopped broccoli into this mixture for 2 hours. Drain and mix in with arugula. Drizzle additional marinade onto vegetables if desired, and garnish with chopped walnuts and Gomasio (see Seasoning Powders).

Waldorf Salad

4 apples, peeled, cored,
and chopped into small pieces
4 stalks celery, minced
2 green onions, minced
1/2 cup chopped walnuts
1/4 cup raisins, soaked for 1 hour

Mix all ingredients in a bowl and set aside. Make and fold in Waldorf Mayonnaise (see below).

Waldorf Mayonnaise

1/2 cup pine nuts, soaked 6 hours
1/4 cup water
2–3 Tbs olive oil
1–2 Tbs lemon juice
Dash of garlic powder
Dash of onion powder
Celtic sea salt to taste

To make mayonnaise place all ingredients into a Vita-Mix and blend until smooth. If too thick, then add a little water. Carefully fold into salad mixture. Serves 4.

Waldorf Salad #2

1 1/2 cups diced apples
1/2 cup minced celery
1/2 cup minced red onions
1/2 cup chopped walnuts
1/2 cup Macadamia Nut Cream
(see Yogurt, Creams, and Cheeses)
1/4 cup raisins, soaked 1 hour
Pinch of Celtic sea salt

Mix all ingredients together and chill. Serve on individual plates with large whole pieces of red lettuce leaves. Place a scoop of Waldorf mixture in the center of each leaf. Garnish with edible flowers. Serves 4.

Sunflower Basil Salad

¼ cup grated zucchini

¼ cup grated squash
(any orange squash)

¼ cup grated jicama

2 cups sunflower sprouts, chopped

2 cups firmly packed fresh basil

3 green onions, sliced thin

3 tomatoes, chopped
into bite-size pieces

½ cup sunflower seeds,
soaked overnight

1 large avocado, cubed

2 garlic cloves, minced

½ tsp minced ginger

¼ tsp minced jalapeño
or dash of cayenne (optional)

3 Tbs olive oil

1 Tbs lemon juice

1 tsp Celtic sea salt, Nama Shoyu,
or Bragg's to taste

1 tsp onion powder

Mix all ingredients into a large bowl, adding spices, oil, and lemon juice last. Serve chilled. Serves 6.

Mexican Creamed Corn Salad

2 corn on cob

½ cup soaked pine nuts

½ cup soaked cashew nuts

1 cup young coconut water

1–2 tsp minced jalapeño

2 thinly sliced scallions

2 cloves garlic, pressed

Sea salt to taste

Cilantro

Blend soaked nuts with coconut water, and add in jalapeño and garlic. Set aside in a bowl. Cut corn from the cob and mix in scallions. Stir into nut cream mixture. Garnish with cilantro. Serves 4.

Caesar Salad

2 hearts of romaine. chopped
½ cup red onion, sliced thin in julienne strips
½–¾ cup Pine Nut Parmesan Cheese (see Yogurt, Creams, and Cheeses)
¼–½ cup Lemon Vinaigrette dressing (see Marinades and Dressings)

Chop romaine leaves into bite-size pieces. Spin-dry in a salad spinner. Mix romaine with onion and toss with Lemon Vinaigrette dressing. Lastly, sprinkle in the Pine Nut Parmesan. Serves 4.

Mixed Sprout Salad

2 cups loosely packed buckwheat sprouts
2 cups largely chopped sunflower sprouts
2 cups mixed alfalfa, clover, and radish sprouts
1 cup mixed lentil mung bean and pea sprouts

This salad mix is the top in enzymes and youth hormones, as it consists of primarily young sprouts. I like to serve this with a creamy dressing, but any of the dressings or sauces would be appropriate. You can also use other sprout combinations. See section on sprouting.

This salad is simple. Just mix the different kinds of sprouts together. Broccoli sprouts are new on the market and are supposed to be excellent for cancer prevention, so you could add some of these or substitute for the radish or alfalfa. When using mung bean sprouts, sprout them for three to four days so they are still relatively small (as opposed to the kind that you buy in the store, which have been sprouted to full maturity). Serve with your favorite dressing and garnish with chopped cherry tomatoes. Serves 4.

Asian Arame Salad

2 cups arame, soaked until soft

½ cup minced green onions

1 cup chopped tomatoes

1 cup peeled and chopped cucumber

*1 large red bell pepper,
cut in thin slices*

*1 cup chopped yellow zucchini,
cut in thin slices*

1–2 cloves garlic, crushed

1 tsp minced ginger

Pinch of cayenne

¼ cup olive oil

¼ cup lemon juice

Arame is a seaweed that is found in the Asian section of health food stores.

Soak arame seaweed overnight or until soft. Strain and rinse well. Place in a bowl and add all the other ingredients. Mix well and chill. Serves 3–4.

*1 green Hawaiian papaya
or ½ green Mexican papaya, grated
(approximately 2 cups)*

*1 cup firm ripe papaya,
peeled and cut julienne*

*1 Golden Delicious apple,
cored and cut julienne*

1 red onion, cut julienne

*2 persimmons (the crunchy kind),
peeled and cut julienne (optional)*

1 large red bell pepper, cut julienne

¼ cup sesame oil

¼ cup olive oil

¼ cup lime juice or lemon juice

2 Tbs agave syrup or honey

1 Tbs minced lemon grass

2 Tbs minced lime leaves

2–3 cloves garlic

2 tsp minced ginger

1 tsp cumin

1 tsp turmeric

1–2 tsp minced Thai chile pepper

½ cup fresh mint, loosely packed

*½ cup chopped peanuts (soak these
overnight, marinate in Nama Shoyu,
then dehydrate until crispy)*

**A Thai specialty that is loaded with living enzymes
and is so good for digestion.**

Slice into thin strips papaya, apple, persimmon, bell pepper, and onion. Make a dressing from blending the oil, lime juice, agave syrup, garlic, ginger, chili, lemon grass, and lime leaves. Blend well and add to the other ingredients. Carefully fold in your mint leaves and peanuts. Serve in individual cabbage leaves with thin slices of avocado on top. They can be picked up and eaten just like a burrito. Serves 4.

Moroccan Vegetable Tagine

1 sweet yellow onion, cubed

4 zucchini, sliced thinly

1 yellow bell pepper, sliced in strips

2 cups diced tomatoes

1½ tsp paprika

1½ tsp cumin

1 tsp each of turmeric, cinnamon, and ginger (use powder form)

¼–½ tsp cayenne or jalapeño

⅛ tsp cardamom

2½ cups miso broth (3 Tbs miso to 2½ cups water)

2 Tbs Sun-Dried Tomato Paste (see Sauces and Dips)

Celtic sea salt to taste

Marinate onions, zucchini, and bell peppers in liquid overnight. Strain carefully and reserve liquid for another occasion. Add in fresh tomatoes, seasonings, and Sun-Dried Tomato Paste. Serve on a bed of mixed sprouts (sunflower, buckwheat, mung, and clover) or Angel Hair Pasta (see Entrées). Garnish with chopped black olives and fresh cilantro. Serves 4–6.

Cucumber à la Mint

2 cucumbers

1 cup Sour Cream (see Yogurt, Creams, and Cheeses)

1 cup soaked raisins

2 Tbs fresh mint leaves

Celtic sea salt to taste

Dash of cayenne

Peel cucumbers and slice very thin. Add sour cream, raisins, mint, salt, and cayenne. Chill for 2 hours. Serves 4.

Sauerkrauts

These are some of the most wonderful sources of friendly bacteria, as they are a fermented food and will keep well in the fridge if stored in a glass container. It's wise to eat some kind of fermented food each day to keep the friendly bacteria in the colon healthy. The other fermented foods on a raw-food diet are your seed cheeses, crackers, and rejuvelac.

Green/Purple Kraut

Green or purple cabbage—2 medium-size heads

Remove the outer leaves and save. Cut the rest of the cabbage up so that it will feed through a Champion juicer with the blank in place. You can grind all of the cabbage or grind one half and shred the other half. Mix together then place in a glass bowl or crock. Knead the mixture with your hands so that it is all uniformly combined. Place the reserved cabbage leaves over the mixture to cover it completely. Place a plate over all of this and set a rock or heavy object on the plate to compress the mixture. Cover with a tea towel and let sit at room temperature for three days. Stir mixture once a day to combine juices. After three days, remove the leaves and any scum that may have formed. If there is a lot of juice on the top, save for marinating mushrooms or other veggies, or use as a base in your salad dressings instead of vinegar. This will keep in the fridge for about two weeks.

Variations:

1) Green Kraut

Add to green cabbage mixture 3 cloves of garlic, grated finely; 2 Tbs fresh dill, minced; and 1 Tbs kelp or Celtic sea salt to taste.

2) Beet Ginger Kraut

1 large head of purple cabbage, 1 beet, 4 stalks of celery, 1 inch of ginger root, and dulse or Celtic sea salt to taste.

Run half of the ingredients through the Champion, and finely chop or shred the remaining ingredients. Proceed as in the basic kraut.

3) Carrot Kraut

1 large head of green cabbage, 3–4 carrots, 1 onion, 2–3 garlic cloves, curry powder, and Celtic sea salt to taste.

These krauts will last forever in the fridge and are a nice complement to your sushi fillings, or as a side dish.

Entrées

Remember that items printed with an initial capital letter, like Tomato Powder, indicate recipes found in this book. See the appropriate sections.

Spinach Nut Burger on a Bun

2 handfuls baby spinach

1 cup ground pumpkin seeds, walnuts, pecans, or almonds

½ cup ground sesame seeds (grind in coffee grinder)

½ cup minced celery

1 cup carrot pulp

¼ cup carrot juice

3 Tbs flax meal

2 Tbs minced parsley

2 Tbs minced red bell pepper

½ cup minced onion

1 tsp Celtic sea salt

Marinate spinach overnight in a mixture of equal parts lemon juice and olive oil. Strain and combine with the remaining ingredients. If mixture is too dry, add more carrot juice. Form into patties and place on dehydrator teflex sheet. Dehydrate 6 hours on one side then flip over and dehydrate for another 6 hours. If you want your burger well done, then leave in longer and test to your liking. Makes 8–10 patties.

Variation: Spinach Nut Cheeseburger

Follow directions above but add a Cheese Patty (see Yogurt, Creams, and Cheeses).

Burger Buns

4 portobello mushrooms about
4 inches in diameter
¼ cup olive oil
¼ cup Bragg's Liquid Aminos

Quite different from the standard hamburger buns, this one offers a whole new dimension to what a burger bun can be.

Cut the stems from the mushrooms and gently scoop some of the center out so that the burger will fit between two mushrooms. Brush the inside and outside of the mushroom with the combined olive oil and Bragg's. Dehydrate on mesh sheets for 6 hours then turn over and dehydrate another 6 hours. Remove from dehydrator and start to build your burger.

Add a spoonful of raw Mayonnaise to your mushroom cap, followed by a leaf of butter lettuce, then your burger patty, and a spread of Bar-B-Q Sauce (see Sauces and Dips). Garnish with a nice thick slice of tomato and a very thin slice of red onion.

Veggi Burger

1 Tbs Tomato Powder
(see Seasoning Powders)
2 tomatoes
1 cup ground-up flax seeds
1 cup walnuts, coarsely ground
2 red bell peppers
2 cups chopped mushrooms
½ medium onion, minced
3 cloves garlic
2 Tbs fresh minced oregano
3 Tbs fresh minced basil
1 tsp minced jalapeño (optional)
2 Tbs Bragg's or 1 tsp Celtic sea salt

Similar to the Spinach Nut Burger, this veggie burger can be served on a Burger Bun (see above) or placed on a large romaine leaf and eaten that way.

In a blender or food processor, blend tomatoes with Tomato Powder, bell peppers, and mushrooms. Add in the rest of the ingredients. Form into patties no thicker than 1 inch and dehydrate 8 hours on one side and 6 hours on the other. Serve warm on a bed of romaine lettuce. Garnish with a thick slice of tomato, sweet onion, Bar-B-Q Sauce, and Mayonnaise (see Sauces and Dips).

Cabbage leaves

Stuffings:
Wild Rice Salad
Rainbow Slaw or
Quinoa Pistachio Salad
(see Salads)

For this recipe save the leftover cabbage leaves from making sauerkrauts. If you don't have these on hand, carefully separate the outer leaves on a head of cabbage and put them into hot water to soften, or marinate them in any of the marinades overnight. If using green cabbage, try to contrast the color of the filling to complement the presentation. Do the same if using the purple cabbage.

Cut the hard stem out of each leaf and fill with Wild Rice, Rainbow Slaw, or Quinoa Salad. Invent your own fillings.

When stuffing cabbage leaves, overlap the base of the leaves where you have cut out the stem. Place about two tablespoons of filling along this edge and start to roll the leaf. Tighten the leaf as you go along, until you come to the end. Secure with a toothpick. Garnish with a sauce or dressing of your choice.

Stuffed Bell Peppers

3 red or yellow bell peppers or a combination of the two

1 zucchini, grated

1 cup of corn

½ cup chopped sunflower sprouts (these are the young green sunflower sprouts)

1 green onion, minced

2 cloves garlic, pressed

1 cup minced cucumber

½ avocado or 3 Tbs olive oil

3 Tbs walnuts or almonds, ground until mealy

2 Tbs flax meal

1 tsp Celtic sea salt, Bragg's, or Nama Shoyu to taste

1 Tbs minced fresh basil

1 Tbs lemon juice

Pinch of cayenne

Garnish, 1 recipe Papaya Seed Vinaigrette

This versatile dish can be made by using different ingredients in your recipe. These are only guidelines, and I invite you to try adding your own ingredients.

Prepare peppers by cutting in half and scooping out the seeds. Arrange on a nice platter. Prepare the nut and seed meals by grinding in a coffee grinder the amount that you need. If you use soaked seeds, then dehydrate well before grinding; otherwise just use the raw seeds. Combine the oil with the seed meal or mash in avocado. Add to this mixture the rest of the ingredients and stuff the peppers. Garnish with a slice of tomato on top and serve on a bed of greens, with Papaya Seed Vinaigrette. Serves 4–6.

Note: Remember to stay away from green bell peppers. This is like a green fruit, and the enzymes are not yet formed, so digesting these can be very difficult.

105

Pink Salmon Loaf
with Creamy Curry Sauce

2 cups soaked almonds

2 medium carrots

1 cup minced celery

½ cup finely chopped green onions

¼ cup carrot juice

1–2 Tbs minced parsley

2–3 Tbs lemon juice

2 tsp kelp

Dash of Nama Shoyu, Bragg's, or Celtic sea salt to taste

Curry to taste (optional)

2–3 cloves garlic, pressed

Sauce:

1 recipe Creamy Curry Sauce

Peel and cut carrots into 1-inch chunks. Alternate a few almonds then a chunk of carrot through the Champion juicer with the blank in place. This will prevent the nuts from backing up or getting too hot as they pass through the housing on the juicer.

Cut the celery into very finely minced pieces, along with the parsley and onion. Add to the almond/carrot mixture. Add your seasonings and enough carrot and lemon juice to moisten the entire mixture. Find a nice oval platter and shape your loaf into a fish. You can get pretty decorative with this if you want to add scales or fins. Be creative. Serve with Creamed Curry Sauce. The leftovers, when made into veggie patties and dehydrated, make wonderful burgers.

Zucchini Orange Pecan Loaf

2 cups soaked pecans
2 zucchini, chopped
1 cup minced celery
½ cup minced onion
¼ cup minced parsley
¼–½ cup fresh-squeezed orange juice with pulp
3 Tbs olive oil
2 Tbs flax meal
2 cloves garlic, pressed
1 tsp minced ginger
Pinch of cayenne or jalapeño (optional)
1 tsp Celtic sea salt

A hearty meal in itself.

Alternate pecans and zucchini chunks through the Champion, with the blank in place. Soak flax seed in orange juice to make a thin paste. Add all the other ingredients and shape into a loaf. You can serve as is or dehydrate by shaping it into a loaf no more than 1½ inches high on a teflex sheet. Dehydrate until a crust forms on the outside. The inside will still be moist. Flip it over by taking another dehydrator tray, placing it on top of the loaf, and quickly flipping both trays so that the loaf is now on the new tray. This is excellent served with Macadamia Nut Cream Sauce. (See Yogurt, Creams, and Cheeses.)

Mushroom Walnut Loaf

2 cups walnuts, soaked 4–6 hours
2 cups chopped mushrooms
3 medium carrots
1 onion
4 stalks celery, minced finely
¼ cup ground flax seeds
2 cloves garlic
2 Tbs minced fresh parsley
½ tsp minced ginger
¼ tsp minced jalapeño
3 Tbs olive oil
1 Tbs Nama Shoyu, Bragg's, or Celtic sea salt to taste
Coco water or orange juice

Another mock meat loaf that is rich in flavor and texture.

Alternate putting walnuts, mushrooms, carrots, and onions through the Champion with the blank in place. You can also use a food processor if you don't have a Champion juicer. Soak flax meal in enough coco water or orange juice to absorb and form a thin paste. Add flax meal and all other ingredients to the mushroom-nut mixture. Knead it all together and form into a loaf. Chill and serve or dehydrate by placing the loaf (about 1½ inches high) on a teflex sheet and dehydrating for 4–6 hours. This makes a nice warm entrée and is delicious served with Sun-Dried Tomato Sauce. Serve on a platter garnished with fresh greens and edible flowers.

Crust:

1 cup almonds, soaked overnight

1 cup pecans, soaked 6 hours

1 tsp Celtic sea salt or 1 Tbs Nama Shoyu or Bragg's

1 Tbs ground flax meal

1 tsp garlic powder

1 tsp onion powder

1/4 cup orange juice or coco water

Filling:

4 cups baby spinach leaves, packed tightly

1/4 cup raw tahini, almond butter, or pumpkin seed butter

1/4 cup macadamia nuts, soaked 3 hours

4 cups chopped mushrooms

2 Tbs lime juice or to taste

1 tsp Celtic sea salt or 2 Tbs Nama Shoyu or Bragg's

2 cloves garlic

1/2–1 tsp minced ginger

1/4 tsp jalapeño or cayenne (optional)

Dash of nutmeg

Dash of cardamom

2–3 Tbs flax meal or psyllium to thicken

1/4 cup young coco water

1 recipe Sunflower Beet Sauce (see Sauces and Dips)

Crust: After soaking the nuts, dehydrate them for 1 hour so they are not soggy. In a food processor with the S blade, process the nuts until they are finely ground. Add in the flax seed meal, seasonings, and enough liquid to moisten and hold together the mixture. Press mixture into a pie plate and dehydrate 1–2 hours.

Filling: In a food processor combine spinach, nuts, nut butter, lime juice, mushrooms, seasonings, and water. Add in enough flax meal or psyllium to thicken. Remember that this will continue to firm up with time. Fill the crust with filling and either chill to firm, or place in the dehydrator for 4 hours if you want this to be a warm dish. Garnish with slices of mushrooms to make a decorative pattern on the top of the quiche. This is delicious served with Sunflower Beet Sauce.

Variation: Broccoli Quiche

Follow the instructions for Spinach Mushroom Quiche but instead of spinach use the same amount of broccoli flowerets; and instead of spicing with cinnamon and cardamom, use 3 Tbs of freshly minced dill. All other ingredients are the same.

Easy Tacos

Taco Shell
Refried Beans
Avocado Garnish

This recipe is always a hit at a party. Try making it with almonds instead of sunflower seeds—they are both delicious. Raw tortilla shells can be used (see Tacos #2 on page 111), but you will have to eat them immediately, as the moisture will tend to rehydrate the shells.

Taco Shell

Romaine lettuce leaves

Wash and dry romaine lettuce leaves and arrange on a platter, being careful not to damage them. Prepare the guacamole and set aside.

Refried Beans

2 cups soaked sunflower seeds
2 tomatoes, quartered
¼ small onion
2 cloves garlic
½ tsp cumin
½ tsp chili powder
1 Tbs minced cilantro
1 tsp Celtic sea salt, dulse,
Nama Shoyu, or Bragg's
2 tsp Tomato Powder
or 4 sun-dried tomatoes, soaked
Jalapeño to taste or pinch of cayenne
Lemon or lime juice to taste
(optional)
1 recipe Guacamole (see Sauces)
or Avocado Garnish
(immediately below)
4 cups mixed alfalfa and buckwheat
sprouts and cherry tomatoes,
quartered

I have found that soaked nuts work best here, as most legumes are difficult to digest.

In a Vita-Mix or other food processor, blend all the taco mix ingredients, making sure to put the tomatoes in the Vita-Mix first to make a liquid that will blend up the rest of the ingredients. Sometimes just a touch of lime or lemon juice will bring out the flavors.

To assemble: Spread a layer of the bean mixture on a lettuce leaf, then cover this with a layer of Guacamole or chopped Avocado Garnish (see below). Then place a layer of mixed sprouts on top of that and garnish each taco with about 4 quarters of cherry tomatoes.

Serve with any of the salsas. Makes about 10 tacos.

Avocado Garnish

2–3 firm ripe avocadoes, diced
½ cup minced green onions
¼–½ cup chopped cilantro
2 Tbs lemon juice
Dash of sea salt

Cut avocado in half and remove seed. Gently remove the whole avocado from the skin and dice. Add the rest of the ingredients, folding carefully so that the avocado does not go to mush.

Taco Shell:

*1 cup flax seed
soaked in 2 cups water*

2 cups corn cut from the cob

2 bell peppers, chopped

¼ cup dried Tomato Powder

*2 Tbs Mexican Seasoning Mix
(see Seasoning Powders)*

⅔ cup water

Fillings:

*Refried beans with Guacamole,
Mango or Papaya Salsa, Mexican
Creamed Corn Salad with Avocado
Garnish (see previous recipe)*

A little variation on the Easy Tacos and oh, so good.

Taco Shell: Place water, corn, bell peppers, and seasonings into the Vita-Mix and blend. Add one-half cup flax seed and blend again to crack the seed. Add blended mixture to the remaining flax seed. On a teflex sheet pour 4-inch circles ¼ inch thick. Dehydrate for 6 hours then flip over and dehydrate the underside for another 6 hours. Remove from dehydrator, fold in half, and return to the dehydrator to complete drying.

Serve with your choice of fillings.

111

Enchiladas

For Tortilla, see Wraps section.

Filling:

*Macadamia Nut Seed Cheese
(see Yogurt, Creams, and Cheeses)*

*Sprinkle of minced red Serrano
chile peppers*

Sauce:

*1 recipe Enchilada Sauce
or Molé Sauce (see Sauces and Dips)*

To assemble, fill tortilla with Macadamia Nut Seed Cheese and minced chile peppers. Fold tortilla over and serve with sauce on top.

Chiles Rellenos with Almond Seed Cheese

*Poblano or Anaheim chiles,
or red bell peppers*

Filling:

2 cups Almond Seed Cheese

1 cup chopped cilantro

½ large onion

1 small zucchini

1 red bell pepper

1 large carrot

1 tomato

2 cloves garlic

2 tsp oregano

1 tsp cumin

*½ tsp minced jalapeño
or cayenne to taste*

1–2 Tbs lemon or lime juice

*1 tsp Celtic sea salt, Nama Shoyu,
or Bragg's to taste*

Prepare the filling first before cutting the peppers in half. That way you can see how many peppers you will need.

For the filling, run the onion, zucchini, bell pepper, carrot, tomato, and garlic through the Champion with the blank in place. You can also try this in a food processor; or simply using a knife, mince the vegetables. Add all the other ingredients and mix well. Adjust flavorings to your taste. I like lots of cayenne or jalapeño when I make this recipe.

Now cut your pepper in half or lengthwise and stuff with the filling. Dehydrate for 10 hours. Serve warm with Nut Creams, Molé Sauce, Papaya Salsa, or Sour Cream.

Tamales with Mango Salsa

6 corn husks

Filling:
Almond Seed Cheese
Refried Beans
Black olives (best when ordered from Rawfood.com—see Resources list)
Garnish with Mango Salsa

Cut corn husks in half and place a large spoonful of bean mixture on each husk, followed by a spoonful of Almond Seed Cheese and chopped olives. Sprinkle with a little chili powder. Pinch ends of husks together to make a little boat-like shape, leaving the filling exposed to dehydrate. Dehydrate for 4 hours and serve with Mango Salsa (see Salsas).

Chiles Rellenos with Almond Seed Cheese

Stuffed Beefsteak Tomatoes with Pesto and Angel Hair Pasta

3 beefsteak tomatoes
1 recipe Pine Nut Basil Seed Cheese
1 recipe Basic Pesto
1 recipe Angel Hair Pasta (see below)
Crispy Garlic Chips

Slice tomatoes nice and thick. Spread a thick layer of seed cheese between two slices of tomato. Place some pasta on a plate, top with your stuffed tomato, and then put a scoop of pesto on top of the tomato and a few dollops on top of the pasta (or serve pesto on the side). Sprinkle with Crispy Garlic Chips (see Seasoning Powders). Serves 4.

Angel Hair Pasta

2 large zucchinis, cut into 3-inch chunks

Using a Saladacco (See Food Preparation Basics), make enough pasta for 4 servings and set aside.

Stuffed Portobello Mushrooms

2 large portobello mushrooms
1 recipe Simple Marinade
1 recipe Almond Seed Cheese
2 green onions, minced
2 cloves garlic, minced
1 tsp minced ginger
½ cup fresh basil, minced
1–2 Tbs minced fresh oregano
Celtic sea salt, Bragg's, or Nama Shoyu to taste

Marinate the mushrooms for 6 hours in the marinade. Turn over regularly to cover all surfaces. Mix the remaining ingredients together and stuff mushrooms. Dehydrate 6–8 hours. Garnish with minced basil. Serve warm with a salad of mixed baby greens and Papaya Vinaigrette dressing. Garnish with Crispy Garlic Chips (see Seasoning Powders). Serves 2.

Noodles:

1 large eggplant or 4 large zucchini, sliced very thin on a mandolin or slicer.

Sauce:

1 recipe Marinara Sauce

Marinated Veggies:

2 portobello mushrooms, sliced thin
2 red bell peppers, sliced thin
1 yellow zucchini
1 green zucchini
1 onion, sliced into rings
1½ cups Bragg's or Nama Shoyu

Cheese:

1 cup macadamia nuts, soaked 6 hours
1 cup pine nuts, soaked 6 hours
¼ cup lemon juice
2–3 cloves garlic
1 tsp Celtic sea salt, Nama Shoyu, or Bragg's to taste
¼ tsp dried hot chile peppers
Water

Noodles: First marinate overnight in Marinara Sauce, enough to coat each side. Let sit in the fridge.

Sauce: Make 1 recipe of Marinara Sauce. I like to add 2 soaked Medjool dates or a little honey to this recipe to give it some sweetness, but this is optional. This is the sauce you use to marinate the noodles.

Marinated Vegetables: Marinate thinly sliced portobello mushrooms, zucchinis, bell peppers, and onion rings in Nama Shoyu or Bragg's Liquid Aminos for 4 hours. Use enough marinade to cover. You want approximately 4 cups of sliced veggies.

Cheese: To make cheese, place all ingredients into the Vita-Mix and blend well. Add enough water to just keep the mixture turning over onto the blades. You want this to be a thick consistency but blended up well.

In a shallow glass baking pan or pie plate, put a layer of noodles in the bottom and bring up along the sides. Spread a little Marinara Sauce on top. Place a layer of cheese on top of sauce, then place a layer of marinated vegetables on top of cheese. Make sure to spread the cheese and vegetables out evenly. Repeat this procedure, ending with a third layer of noodles. Dehydrate for 8–10 hours. Serves 6–8.

115

After eating these pizzas you will never want to eat a store-bought pizza again. The crust provides essential fatty acids (omega-3s and omega-6s), and the texture is very much like a conventional pizza. There are many toppings to choose from, and you can come up with some of your own.

Crust:

2 cups buckwheat, soaked overnight and sprouted two days
1 cup flax seeds
1 cup carrot pulp
1 tsp garlic powder
1 tsp basil
1 tsp oregano
¼ cup olive oil

Pizza Crust

Mix all ingredients in a bowl. Divide into four parts and put one part at a time in the Vita-Mix or blender and blend until dough is formed. Empty contents into another bowl. Repeat with the other three portions. Stir the entire mixture together so that it is uniform. Take some scoops of the mixture and place on each teflex sheet in the dehydrator, spreading the mixture out to form pizza circles, no more than ¼ inch thick. Make some large circles and some smaller ones. That way if you are just making one for yourself or for a larger party then you have a choice. Dehydrate at 95 degrees for approximately 8 hours, then remove teflex by placing another tray on top and flipping the whole thing over. Dehydrate the underside for another 8 hours. You want these nice and dry so they will store well. You can store these loosely wrapped in foil and placed in a cool dry area. They should last approximately one month.

Sauce:

*1 recipe Marinara Sauce
or 1 recipe Pesto Sauce (Basic Pesto
or Sun-Dried Tomato Pesto)*

Pizza Sauce: Choose from the one of the sauces. Make recipe and set aside.

Cheese:

½ cup macadamia nuts, soaked 6 hours
½ cup pine nuts, soaked 6 hours
¼ cup fresh parsley, chopped
*½ tsp Celtic sea salt, Nama Shoyu,
or Bragg's*
¼ tsp freshly ground black pepper
¼ cup lemon juice
Water

Cheese: Blend all ingredients, adding just enough water to keep blades turning. Set aside half the cheese mixture for later.

Spread a layer of cheese over the pizza crust about ¼ inch thick. Spread a layer of pizza sauce on top of that. Add your toppings—see below.

Toppings:

Onion rings, sliced ¼ inch thick
Red bell peppers, sliced ¼ inch thick
Mushrooms, sliced ¼ inch thick
*Miniature zucchini or squashes,
sliced ¼ inch thick*
Bragg's Liquid Aminos

Pizza Toppings: Slice enough of the vegetables to spread over the pizza you are preparing. Marinate in Bragg's to soften, approximately 4 hours. Squeeze the marinade out and arrange the vegetables over the cheese layer. Drop teaspoonfuls of the remaining cheese over the topping and garnish (see below).

Garnish:

½ cup minced tomatoes
¼ cup minced red bell peppers
*¼ cup minced green onions
or sweet onion*
2 Tbs minced fresh basil
2 Tbs minced fresh oregano
1 Tbs fresh rosemary, minced very fine
½ tsp dried chile pepper seeds
½ tsp minced garlic
Edible flowers

Garnish: For garnishing the pizzas, first sprinkle the tomatoes over the top, then sprinkle the bell peppers and onions. Next mix the herbs together and sprinkle those on top. If you want to warm in the dehydrator, place on a tray for 30 minutes then serve. To make this festive, garnish with edible flowers.

Variation: Pizza Mexicano

Crust: Use recipe for Mexican Flax Crackers (see Croutons, Bread, Crackers, and Granolas). Add ¼ cup olive oil to recipe and dehydrate, making round circles about 5–6 inches in diameter. Dehydrate both sides at 95 degrees until thoroughly dry. Store in cool dry place until ready to use.

Toppings: Spread a layer of mock Refried Beans (see Easy Tacos, above) over surface of pizza crusts. Follow with a layer of Guacamole (see Sauces).

Garnish with a mixture of the following: diced red bell peppers, diced Roma tomatoes, minced red onion, and chopped cilantro. Drop small amounts of Papaya Salsa or Tropical Salsa (see Salsas) over the top of the pizza and sprinkle with chopped black olives. Squeeze a little lime juice over pizza before serving.

Arabian Pizza

Crust:
1 recipe Pizza Italiano Crust (above)

Toppings:
*1 recipe Hummus
(see Sauces and Dips)*
*1 recipe Cucumber à la Mint
(see Salads)*
⅓ cup sprouted quinoa (optional)

Garnish:
*? tsp Moroccan Hot Sauce
(see Sauces and Dips)*

Spread a layer of Hummus over pizza crust. Follow with a layer of Cucumber à la Mint. Sprinkle with sprouted quinoa. Garnish with Moroccan Hot Sauce. (Be careful, as this is very hot!)

Noodles:

2 medium green zucchini

1 yellow zucchini, julienned

1 small onion, sliced into rings

1 portobello mushroom, sliced into thin strips

1 red bell pepper, julienned

½ cup basil, sliced into thin strips

3 Tbs fresh oregano leaves

2 tsp minced fresh rosemary

2 Tbs tarragon leaves

1 cup tomatoes, diced and pressed to remove excess juices

2 Tbs lime juice

1 tsp minced garlic

½ tsp powdered chile pepper seeds

Simple Marinade

1 recipe Marinara Sauce

Garnish:

Pine Nut Parmesan (see Yogurt, Creams, and Cheeses)

This recipe is an Italian favorite. You can simplify the process by making your noodles with the Saladacco. If you choose to do this, use chunks of zucchini for making your pasta.

Marinate yellow zucchini, onion rings, mushrooms, and bell pepper for 4 hours to soften in Simple Marinade. Drain and save marinade for another occasion. Slice green zucchini on a mandolin, or shave with a potato peeler to make noodles. Add in marinated vegetables and all other ingredients.

Make Marinara Sauce and serve on a platter with noodles. Garnish with Pine Nut Parmesan. Serve with Garlicky Bread (see Side Dishes). Serves 4.

119

Indian Vegetable Curry

2 small green zucchini, sliced very thin lengthwise on a mandolin or with a potato peeler

2 small yellow zucchini, sliced very thin lengthwise on a mandolin or shaved with a potato peeler

1 small yellow zucchini, sliced ¼ inch thick into round disks

2 small carrots, shaved with potato peeler

1 carrot, cut into julienne strips

1 red bell pepper, cut julienne

1 yellow bell pepper, cut julienne

1 small red onion, sliced very thin into strips

⅔ cup corn kernels

½ cup marinated mushrooms (optional)

⅔ cup loosely packed spinach, cut in thin strips

1 young coconut with rubbery spoon meat in it

¼ jicama, cut julienne

1 cup cherry tomatoes

¼ cup raisins

1 apple, cut julienne

¼ cup chopped scallions

2 Tbs lemon or lime juice

1 recipe Orange Vinaigrette (see Marinades and Dressings)

1 tsp Indian Spice Mix (see Seasoning Powders)

1 recipe Curry Sauce (see Sauces and Dips)

Garnish:

Yogurt and Spicy Cashew Croutons (optional)

This is a fabulous dish if you like curry. It is not too hot and has a unique blend of flavors. Enjoy!

Using a potato peeler, shave zucchini and carrots into thin strips. Dice or chop the soft center. Slice the bell peppers into thin strips, along with the apple, spinach, and coconut meat. Reserve half of the bell peppers and set aside.

Add the corn, raisins, cherry tomatoes, and scallions to the shaved zucchini, carrots, bell pepper, apple, spinach, and coconut meat mixture.

Make Orange Vinaigrette and add 1 tsp Indian Spice Mix to it.

Marinate the reserved bell peppers, sliced mushrooms, yellow zucchini rounds, and red onions in the Orange Marinade for 2–3 hours to soften. Strain vegetables from marinade and add to the rest of the vegetables just before serving.

Make the curry sauce and drizzle over vegetables just before serving. Garnish with yogurt (see Yogurt section) and chopped Spicy Cashew Croutons (see Croutons, Bread, Crackers, and Granolas). Serves 4–6.

Shishkabobs with Teriyaki Sauce

Mushroom caps
Cherry tomatoes
Zucchini slices
Orange bell peppers
Red onion pieces
1 recipe Herbed Vinaigrette
(see Marinades and Dressings)
Romaine lettuce
Teriyaki Sauce (see Sauces and Dips)

Marinate all the vegetables in marinade overnight in the fridge. Place onto skewer, brush with a little Bragg's or Nama Shoyu, and dehydrate for 10 hours or to taste. Serve on a romaine lettuce leaf with Teriyaki Sauce, Creamy Tahini Dressing, or "Peanut" Sauce.

Zucchini Torte
with Mexican Creamed Corn Salad

3 large zucchini sliced thin
on the mandolin
2 large red bell pepper, cut julienne
1 small red onion, cut julienne
2 corn on cob
2 jalapeño chiles,
cut, seeded, and minced
1 recipe Macadamia Nut Cream
(make thick)
1–2 Tbs flax meal
1 recipe Simple Marinade
Garnish with chopped cilantro

Slice zucchini, bell peppers, and onions and pour Simple Marinade over them. Marinate overnight in the fridge. Cut corn from the cob and mix with minced chiles. Drain marinated vegetables and mix in Macadamia Nut Cream and flax meal. Place a layer of vegetables in the bottom of a pie plate, followed by a layer of corn niblets and another layer of zucchini noodles. Sprinkle cilantro on top and dehydrate for 6 hours. Serve warm with Mexican Creamed Corn Salad (see Salads).

Shishkabobs with Teriyaki Sauce

Pad Thai Noodles with "Peanut" Sauce

Pad Thai Noodles with "Peanut" Sauce

Noodles:

2 young coconuts

⅓ red onion, cut julienne

1 carrot, shaved with potato peeler

½ red bell peppers, cut julienne

3 red cabbage leaves, rolled and sliced very thinly

½ cup yellow zucchini, cut julienne

½ cup green zucchini, cut julienne

¼ cup chopped cilantro

1 small sweet chile pepper, cut julienne

Thai food lovers, this one is for you!

Remove the young coconut meat from the shells and cut into strips. Prepare the rest of the vegetables and set aside.

Pad Thai Sauce

1 recipe Ginger Shoyu Sauce

2 Tbs Tamarind Puree (see Sauces and Dips)

1 tsp minced Serrano chile

1 recipe "Peanut" Sauce

Garnish:

Spicy Cashew Croutons

Combine Ginger Shoyu Sauce with Tamarind Puree and minced Serrano chile. Blend all together until smooth.

To assemble, carefully mix Pad Thai Sauce with all the above vegetables. Serve with "Peanut" Sauce and garnish with Spicy Cashew Croutons (see Croutons, Bread, Crackers, and Granolas). Serves 4.

125

Side Dishes

Carrot Beet Pâté

4 peeled carrots
1 beet, chopped
1 cup sunflower seeds, soaked overnight
1/2 cup almonds, soaked overnight and then blanched
1/2 cup red onion, chopped
1/2 cup minced red bell peppers
2 Tbs minced parsley
1 Tbs Bragg's Liquid Aminos
2 Tbs lemon juice
2 cloves garlic

Pâtés make a quick and easy filling for wraps and rolls or as a stuffing for vegetables. They are made up of a blend of mixed vegetables, soaked seeds or nuts, and spices. To make one, all you do is run the ingredients through the Champion juicer with the blank attachment, mix it throughly, and then store it in the fridge.

Run the carrots, beet, nuts, garlic, and onion through the Champion with the blank in place. Add the lemon juice, Bragg's, bell pepper, and parsley. Mix well and keep chilled.

Stuffed Mushrooms

12 large mushroom caps
Stems from these mushrooms
1/2 onion, minced
1/4 cup parsley, minced
1 tsp Celtic sea salt or 2 tsp Nama Shoyu
1/2 cup walnuts, Macadamia Nut Cream, or Hummus (or seed cheese)
2 Tbs lemon juice
Olive oil to moisten (optional)
1 tsp Mixed Italian Seasoning (see Seasoning Powders)

These make wonderful appetizers. You can also use any leftover hummus, nut creams, or nut loafs with this recipe.

Clean mushrooms carefully and brush both sides with a combination of olive oil and lemon juice. (The oil and lemon are not included in the amounts above, so be prepared to use a little extra.) Prepare filling by placing all ingredients in the food processor. If too dry, use olive oil to moisten or a little water.

Stuff mushrooms generously and place on dehydrator trays. Dehydrate for 8 hours. Serve warm.

Couscous

3 large parsnips, grated
1 cup pine nuts, soaked overnight
¼ tsp saffron
¼ tsp cumin
½ cup pistachios
½ cup raisins, soaked 2 hours
Garnish, Moroccan Hot Sauce

This is the raw version of the popular Far Eastern staple.

Rinse and dehydrate pine nuts until dry and crunchy. They will not be as crunchy as other nuts due to their high oil content. Place ½ cup of pine nuts in the food processor with parsnips, saffron, and cumin. Process until granulated. Add the pistachios, the rest of the pine nuts, and the soaked raisins. Serve with Moroccan Hot Sauce.

Scrambled Eggs & Bacon

"Bacon":
1 recipe Mock Bacon
(see p. 134)

"Eggs":
2 corn on the cob
1 cup grated cauliflower
½ cup minced red bell pepper
¼ cup minced scallions
⅓ cup minced parsley
1 tsp cumin
1 tsp tumeric
2 cloves minced garlic
¼ cup olive oil
Squeeze of lemon
or lime juice to taste
Dash of Celtic sea salt or Bragg's
Dash of cayenne
Water

Cut corn from the cob and mix all the ingredients together. Add a little water to moisten if necessary. You can heat this dish up ever so slightly in your dehydrator by spreading it out on a teflex sheet for half an hour. Serve warmed with Mock Bacon and any of the salsas.

Stuffed Avocado Boats

Avocados

Stuffing:

Purple Sauerkraut (see Sauerkrauts)

Garnish:

*Herbed Vinaigrette
(see Marinades and Dressings)*

This dish enhances the presentation of any dinner, with its purple contrast against the green of the avocado. The purple sauerkraut is a wonderful source of friendly bacteria that we get from all the fermented foods.

Cut avocados in half and pop out the seed. Brush the avocado with a little lemon juice, and stuff with purple sauerkraut. Drizzle with Herbed Vinaigrette around the sides of avocado and a little on top.

Stuffed Cabbage Boats

1 purple or green cabbage

Stuffing:

*Any Seed Cheese recipe
or filling of your choice
(see Yogurt, Creams, and Cheeses)*

Keep in mind the contrasting colors of your stuffing choices.

Make sure your cabbage leaves are fresh. Carefully remove them from the cabbage, making sure to keep the whole leaf intact. To do this best, cut the base off first so that the leaves naturally want to separate and fall off. Then run water from the tap into the base of the cabbage, helping to loosen the leaves. These cabbage-leaf containers should resemble small bowls. Fill with any flavored Seed Cheese, pâté, or anything else you might like. Garnish with your choice of vinaigrette or sauce.

Sun-Dried Tomatoes in Olive Oil

1 recipe Simple Marinade
4–6 tomatoes sliced nice and thick
*1 recipe Herbed Olive Oil
(see Marinades and Dressings)*

Slice tomatoes and marinate overnight. Place on teflex sheets and dehydrate both sides until chewy. Place in a glass jar and add Herbed Olive Oil to cover. Keep in fridge indefinitely.

Tropical Mango Chutney

¼ cup fresh pineapple, diced

½ cup fresh young coconut, diced

2 cups mango, diced

½ cup onion, minced

¼ cup lemon juice

6 Medjool dates, soaked 2 hours

¼ cup soaked raisins

1 tsp cumin

½ tsp ginger, minced

Green or red chile to taste
or jalapeño pepper, minced

½ tsp–1 tsp Celtic sea salt
or Nama Shoyu to taste

This makes a wonderful spread for any cracker or raw bread, or a flavorful garnish for an entrée.

Blend lemon juice with dates, or mash dates with lemon juice, making a paste. Add in remaining ingredients and chill. Keeps fresh in the fridge for approximately five days. Makes 3½ cups.

Cilantro Chutney

½ cup coconut, shredded
(fresh or dried). If using fresh
coconuts you will need to buy the
more mature kind.

2 cups cilantro

¼–½ onion, chopped

¼ cup lemon juice

Honey or agave syrup to taste

Green chile or red chile to taste
(fresh is best, so start with
a small amount first)

Cumin to taste

Celtic sea salt or Nama Shoyu to taste

This recipe can be used as a relish or a dip and is especially delicious with Indian dishes.

Blend cilantro with lemon juice in blender or Vita-Mix. Add coconut and chile. Add small amount of water if needed for blending purposes. Add remaining ingredients and blend. Makes 1 cup chutney and will keep for one week in the fridge.

Sun-Dried Tomato Sauce/Paste

½ cup dried tomatoes, soaked,
or Tomato Powder
½ cup onions, chopped
1–2 cloves garlic
1 Tbs lime or lemon juice
¼ cup olive oil
1 Medjool date, soaked
¼ cup sun-dried olives (optional)
Celtic sea salt to taste

This is a good substitute for ketchup or an ingredient to add if you want a real strong tomato flavor in a recipe. This is great served on top of Stuffed Cabbage Rolls or a mock meat loaf.

Place ingredients into the Vita-Mix and blend into a thick sauce, adding more water if necessary to acquire the right consistency. Use the soaking water for this. If making a paste, keep it thick.

Pizza Hors d'oeuvres

6 small zucchinis or 2 large ones
2 cups Basic Fermented Seed Cheese
1 tsp onion powder
or ½ onion, minced
3–4 cloves garlic, minced
1 tsp oregano
1 tsp basil
1–2 tomatoes
2 Tbs Tomato Powder
½ tsp Celtic sea salt, Nama Shoyu,
or Bragg's to taste
Additional tomatoes, approximately 10

These are delicious little snacks that make a good accompaniment to any Italian dish or soup.

Cut zucchini on a diagonal about ¼ inch thick and spread out on the mesh dehydrator sheets. Combine tomatoes, onion, garlic, and spices in the blender and add to the seed cheese, mixing it well. If you want more tomato flavor then add more Tomato Powder (see Seasoning Powders). Adjust the seasoning to your taste also. I like lots of oregano and will add fresh oregano and fresh basil sometimes.

Spread a layer of the seed mixture on the zucchini about ¼ inch thick. Then place a basil leaf on top of the seed cheese or additional minced garlic. Cut additional tomatoes into thick slices, and place one slice on top of each basil leaf. Sprinkle with a little sea salt, dulse, oregano, and/or garlic powder. Dehydrate for 24 hours. These should be a little chewy, like pizza. If you have any leftovers, then store in the fridge. They will last about five days. Serves 4–6.

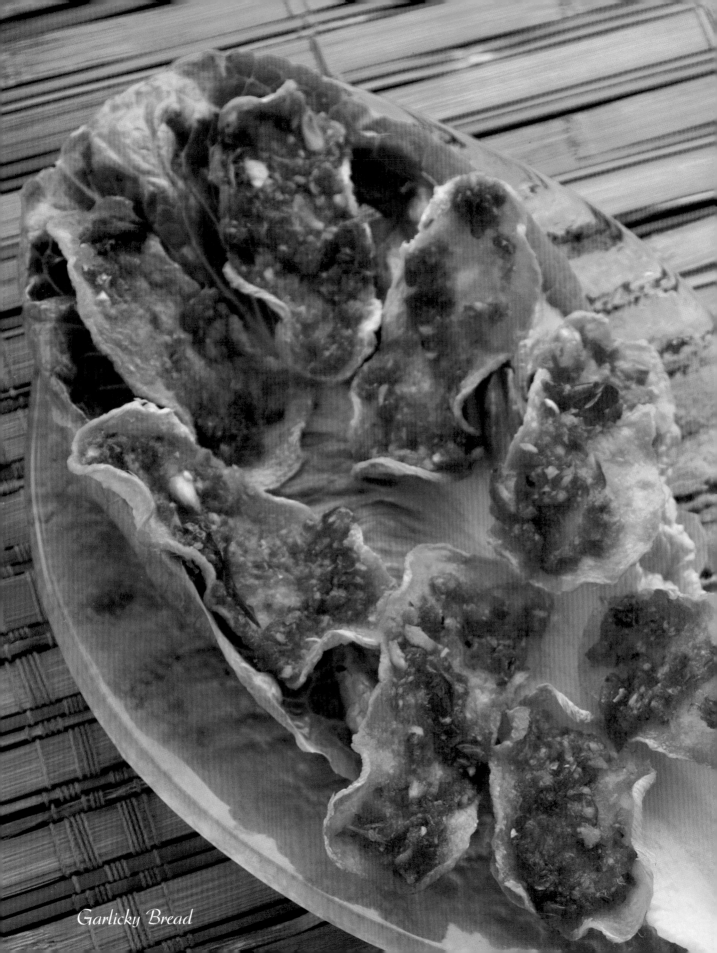

Garlicky Bread

Pickled Ginger

1 cup shaved ginger

Bragg's organic raw apple cider vinegar

1 slice fresh beet for color

This is a pickled ginger similar to the pink slices of pickled ginger you get at a sushi bar.

Peel ginger and shave with a potato peeler into very thin slices. Use the woody interior of the ginger for a later recipe. Place ginger into a glass jar and cover with the vinegar. Place slice of beet in jar. This will add the familiar color. Remove beet when ginger has absorbed the color. This will last quite a while if kept refrigerated. It's delicious served with sushi rolls.

Garlicky Bread

1 jicama

1 red or yellow bell pepper, minced

1 diced tomato, strained

8–10 cloves garlic, minced

1 tsp Celtic sea salt

1/3 cup olive oil

Fresh oregano or basil, minced

These are so good that they never last long. They make great appetizers and a nice accompaniment to any pasta dish. (Adapted from Juliano's *Raw Uncook Book*.)

Slice jicama on a mandolin or other slicing utensil, no more than ¼ inch thick. The thinner the better. Dice tomatoes and strain the juice from them by pressing in a sieve. Mix all the other ingredients together and spread on top of the jicama. Dehydrate on the plastic trays in the dehydrator for 10 hours or until nice and chewy.

Caviar

2 Red Delicious apples
⅓ cup black sesame butter
1 Tbs honey (optional)
Cashew Cream Sauce (see Yogurt, Creams, and Cheeses)

Looks like caviar and tastes even better.

Peel apples and slice into thin rounds ¼ inch thick. Mix sesame butter with honey and spread a thin layer on apple slices. Arrange on a platter of buckwheat sprouts or other greens. This is optional but adds to the presentation. Garnish with Cashew Cream.

Mock Bacon

2–4 coconuts

Marinade:
Nama Shoyu or Bragg's

You won't believe this recipe, and your friends will never guess what this is made from.

The key here is to buy young coconuts like they have in the Asian markets. Or if you live in Mexico like I do, then buy them fresh from the vendors on the street. I buy coconuts in bulk because I use so many in my recipes. Ask for the young spoon-meat kind where the meat inside is not jelly but has a slight rubbery texture to it.

Open the cocos and save the water for soups, sauces, or dressings, or just drink it.

Scoop out the meat and marinate it overnight in a bowl. Add enough Bragg's or shoyu to cover. Dehydrate until dry. These strips of "bacon" will have a rubbery texture when done. They are so delicious and can be chopped up into small pieces (bacon bits) and added to salads, or if they last long enough they can be eaten as snacks.

Caviar

Wraps
and Spring Rolls

Anything that envelops a stuffing we call a wrap. They make a great replacement for the traditional sandwich. They are fast to prepare and so much healthier.

Tortillas #1

Use the same recipe as for Cheese Patties (see Yogurt, Creams, and Cheeses), but omit the yeast, curry, and turmeric. Add 2 Tbs olive oil to the recipe. You can make the circles a little larger, as you will be stuffing these with a filling. Dehydrate at 90 degrees and make sure not to over-dehydrate or the tortillas will crack on you. You want them to feel and look like fruit leathers.

Tortillas #2

If you have any leftover Tomato Basil Soup or Creamy Cilantro Spinach Soup, then simply add a little avocado to make it creamier and follow the instructions above. These should be like fruit leathers that just peel off the teflex sheets.

Sushi Rolls

This makes a wonderful side dish to any entrée or can be eaten as an entrée. It is also a recipe that lends itself to much creativity just by altering the fillings.

How to roll sushi

Place your nori sheets on a clean dry surface. Turn the nori so that the short side is closest to you. Place your dry filling ingredients along the side closest to you. Then add the wetter ingredients on top of this and follow with more dry ingredients. The idea here is not to get the nori sheets damp or they will tear when you start to roll them. Do not fill beyond $\frac{1}{3}$ of the surface area of the nori. It is just fine if your ingredients extend out beyond the edges, as this enhances the presentation. Make sure that the thickness of your filling is even right across the sheet.

Now with dry hands start to roll the sushi by bringing up the edge closest to you and rolling over the filling. Use both hands, tightening down with your fingers as you move along. When you come to the end, seal the edge with a little water, or sometimes I'll use a slice of tomato or cucumber that is still moist to glue the edge. Roll the sushi over so that the seam is facing down, and slice into bite-size pieces using a very sharp serrated knife.

2 sheets raw nori (from Rawfood.com to ensure that it's raw)
4 julienne slices each of carrots, celery, cucumber, green onions
1 thick slice of a large tomato, cut into three strips
3–4 strips of avocado
½ tsp minced garlic (optional)
½ tsp minced ginger (optional)
Dulse flakes (optional)
Buckwheat sprouts or half buckwheat mixed with half alfalfa
4 Tbs seed cheese, nut loaf, or other fillings (see below)
Yellow miso to spread on nori (optional)

Spread a very thin layer of miso on a nori sheet. Next place a few sprouts on the nori, followed by the strips of vegetables. Next spread the seed cheese, nut filling, or whatever you wish to use on top of this. Sprinkle evenly the garlic, dulse, and ginger across the filling. Follow with more sprouts. Roll as above. Cut and serve.

Note: Be careful not to stuff it too much, as you have to be able to roll it. When cutting your sushi use a very sharp knife and put the seam side down.

Sushi Fillings:

Curry Seed Cheese or any of the seed cheese variations, Carrot Beet Pâté, Sauerkraut, Hummus, or Pink Salmon Loaf

With these fillings add the julienned vegetables as suggested in the standard sushi, along with the sprouts. Makes 2 rolls.

*4 sheets of rice flour paper,
8½ inches diameter
(buy at Asian markets)*

4 cups buckwheat sprouts

1 recipe Rainbow Slaw (see Salads)

*1–2 tsp Indian Spice Mix
(see Seasoning Powders)*

½ cup macadamia nut butter

1–2 tsp honey

1 tsp psyllium husk

*Garnish with cherry tomatoes
and Pickled Ginger*

138

These are so good and a party favorite. You could serve them with a Sweet & Sour Sauce, Ginger Shoyu Sauce, or Wasabi, but first try the dipping sauce in this recipe.

Rice paper is a thin translucent wrap that is made from rice (as its name suggests); it can be found in Asian markets and is used for spring rolls in Thai restaurants. Soak rice paper in water until soft and pliable. Lay it down flat on a clean surface and pat dry the top. Place a layer of buckwheat sprouts across the middle of the circle. Strain the Rainbow Slaw so that it is not too wet and save the juices. Then place a layer of Rainbow Slaw on top of the greens. Lightly sprinkle with Indian Spice Mix. Next dribble a thin layer of macadamia nut butter on top of the Rainbow Slaw. Now begin to fold the edge closest to you over the vegetables, tucking in the sides as you go, and continue to roll until you have a cylindrical shape. Make sure that the edges do not curl up on you and that your roll is secure. Make four of these wraps, cut in half with a sharp knife, and serve on a platter with arugula leaves.

Dipping Sauce:

Combine ⅔ of a cup of the juices from the Rainbow Slaw in a blender with the honey, Indian Spice Mix, and psyllium. If you desire more Indian flavor then add a little more spice. Place in a small bowl and arrange in the center of your platter. Serves 4.

Simply Spring Rolls

1 head butter lettuce

Filling:

*1½ cups pecans, soaked and
dehydrated*

¼ small onion, minced

¼ cup lemon juice

2 Tbs honey

1 Tbs water if necessary

*Handful of mint leaves and diced
cucumber, seeded*

1 recipe Creamy Tahini Dressing

Process pecans in food processor until mealy. Remove to a bowl and mix in remaining ingredients. Pat mixture into finger-like patties. Place one patty per leaf of butter lettuce. Add a few mint leaves and some diced cucumber. Roll leaves over the filling and secure with a toothpick. Serve with Creamy Tahini Dressing.

Vietnamese Spring Rolls

*2 sheets rice flour paper,
8½ inches in diameter*

Butter lettuce, 6 leaves

*2 handfuls of buckwheat sprouts
(you can also use mung or alfalfa)*

6 Tbs almond seed cheese

2 long strips daikon radish

2–4 long strips carrot

*½ red or yellow bell pepper,
julienned*

1–2 Tbs beet juice (optional)

*Garnish with Sweet & Sour Sauce
or Ginger Shoyu Sauce*

These rolls are similar to the Rainbow Wraps and can be quite versatile when different fillings are used.

Marinate the bell pepper, carrot, and radish in Simple Marinade (see Marinades and Dressings) for 4 hours. Drain well and pat dry.

Dampen the rice paper with water until soft and pliable. Place on a clean surface or cutting board and pat dry the top. Place one half of the lettuce leaves on the rice paper and follow with marinated vegetables, placing them across the rice paper in a line. Next, spread 3 Tbs of almond seed cheese (that has been mixed with a little beet juice to give it color) on top of the vegetables. If you want to add any seasoning, this is the time to do it. I sometimes will squirt a little Bragg's over this or sprinkle chopped-up garlic. Next, spread a handful of sprouts on top of the vegetables. Now very carefully wrap the rice paper as explained in the above recipe. Cut on a diagonal and garnish with your choice of sauces. Serves 2.

Vegetarian Spring Rolls
with Ginger Shoyu Sauce

Rice paper

Filling:

1 carrot cut in julienne strips

1 zucchini cut in julienne strips

*1 red bell pepper
cut in julienne strips*

*½ sweet onion sliced thinly
into strips*

1 cup finely shredded purple cabbage

½ cup mung bean sprouts

*1 cup baked goat cheese,
or almond seed cheese*

1 recipe Simple Marinade

*1 recipe Ginger Shoyu Sauce
or Sweet & Sour Sauce*

Marinate the carrots, zucchini, bell peppers, and onions for 3 hours. Remove from marinade. Strain vegetables well and pat dry. Fill each circle of rice paper with a combination of the filling ingredients, placing the lengths of the julienne-cut veggies diagonally across the paper, then adding a thin line of goat cheese spread. Start wrapping from one of the corners, folding the side edges over as you go. Stick a toothpick in the roll if necessary to secure. Serve with Ginger Shoyu Sauce or Sweet & Sour Sauce.

Keep the leftover marinade for another occasion. It will last in the fridge for 21 days.

140

Bread

Basic Raw Bread

8 cups vegetable pulp (carrot, beet, zucchini, tomatoes, etc.)
1 cup vegetable juice or more if necessary to moisten
2 cups ground flax seed
1 cup raisins, soaked 4 hours
1 Tbs Celtic sea salt

Want to know what to do with your vegetable pulp leftovers? Try making this Raw Bread recipe. It's a wonderful source of fiber and nutrients and makes the best sandwiches ever. After eating this bread you will never want to go back to the standard bread types. This is so delicious, and you can be creative by adding your favorite spices.

Save your pulp from your fresh-squeezed juices until you have 8 cups. Don't use celery pulp, as it is very stringy. Blend soaked raisins with vegetable juice and sea salt to a smooth consistency. Add to vegetable pulp and massage mixture well. Let it sit in the bowl covered with a tea towel for two days. It will rise slightly. After two days then spread the mixture on your teflex sheets, no more than ½ inch thick. Score into bread-size pieces. Dehydrate at 105 degrees for 6 hours, then flip over to dehydrate the bottom side for another 6 hours. To do this, simply place an empty tray on top of the bread and turn the whole thing over. This bread should be pliable and feel like bread. Separate pieces and wrap in cellophane. When stored in the fridge, it will last for ages.

Flax Crackers

Caraway Seed Rye Bread

*2 cups rye, soaked
and sprouted 2 days*

*1 cup sunflower seeds,
soaked overnight*

½ cup ground flax seed

¼ onion

2 Tbs caraway seed, cracked

1 tsp Celtic sea salt

Alternate running the rye berries and sunflower seeds through the Champion with the blank in place. Repeat this two or three times to make sure that the seeds and grains are ground up well. Place in a bowl and add your flax meal, caraway seed, and sea salt. Mince very finely one quarter of a large onion and add to the mixture. Place on a teflex sheet and mold into a loaf no thicker than 1½ inches. Dehydrate at 90 degrees for 12 hours then flip over to dehydrate the underside. The outside will form a crust and the inside will be moist. Store in the fridge.

Crackers

Rye Crackers

2 cups sprouted rye grain

*1 cup sunflower seeds,
soaked overnight*

½ onion

2 cloves garlic

¼ cup dill weed

1 stalk celery, chopped

¼ cup parsley

2 tsp caraway seeds, ground

½ tsp Celtic sea salt or 1 tsp dulse

Process rye, sunflower seeds, onion, celery, dill, and parsley through the Champion juicer with the blank attachment. Add in dulse or salt last, kneading the mixture well to combine all the ingredients evenly. Run the dough through the Champion a second time to make sure that the rye seeds are crushed well; otherwise when dehydrated these can be hard to chew. Spread onto a teflex sheet and score into cracker-size pieces using the back of a large knife or pizza cutter. Dehydrate for 1–2 days, flipping over if necessary. Serve with your favorite dip or seed cheese.

About Flax Seeds

These tiny seeds are packed full of nutrients and essential fatty acids, particularly the omega-3s. Being strong antioxidants, they provide protection from the sun's radiation, beautify our skin, and strengthen our nervous system and immune system. When soaking flax seeds you need to soak in twice as much water. The seeds will acquire a gelatinous substance around them after soaking, which is difficult to wash off. It is not necessary to do this, as this gel has many nutritional benefits to it and helps to hold the crackers together. See below.

Flax Seed Crackers

3 cups flax seeds, soaked for 4 hours
8 stalks celery
½ onion
4 cloves garlic
1 Tbs kelp powder
1 cup basil
½ cup minced parsley
½ cup water
1 tsp Celtic sea salt
½ tsp cayenne (optional)

Soak flax seeds overnight in twice as much water as seeds. Drain off any excess water but do not rinse the seeds. Cut celery up into smaller pieces and place in the Vita-Mix along with water, onion, garlic, kelp, basil, cayenne, and sea salt. Blend until smooth, then add to flax seeds. Stir mixture well, then add half of the mixture back to the blender and blend to make dough. Add back to remaining whole flax seeds and mix well. Add in the parsley and spread the mixture onto teflex sheets to make a large square approximately ¼ inch thick. Dehydrate at 105 degrees for 12 hours then flip over, remove the teflex sheet carefully, and dry the underneath side, approximately another 12 hours. Break into cracker-size pieces and store in a covered container. If you want more uniform pieces, then after one hour of dehydrating, score the top of the cracker with the back of a large knife enough to make an indentation. When dry, it will break apart at these lines.

Mexican Flax Crackers

Blend three tomatoes, 1 red bell pepper, ½ onion, 3 garlic cloves, 2 tsp chili powder, 2 tsp cumin, ½ tsp cayenne, 1 tsp sea salt, and ½ cup water. Follow the same procedure as above.

Italian Flax Crackers

Blend ½ cup Sun-Dried Tomatoes in Olive Oil (see Side Dishes) with 3 tomatoes, 1 cup fresh basil loosely packed, ¼ cup fresh oregano, 1 Tbs minced rosemary, ½ onion, 3 garlic cloves, 1 tsp sea salt, and ½ cup water. Add this mixture to 3 cups soaked flax seeds. Follow the same procedure as above. Soak seeds 6–8 hours.

Multi-Seed Flax Crackers

This is made the same as the Flax Seed Cracker but add ½ cup soaked sesame seeds, ½ cup soaked pumpkin seeds, and ½ cup soaked sunflower seeds. Increase the water to 1 cup when blending. You can add extra amounts of the other ingredients but it is not necessary.

145

Flax Seed Raisin Crackers

2 cups flax seeds, soaked overnight
1 cup raisins, soaked 4 hours
1/2 cup sesame seeds, soaked 4 hours
1/2 cup fresh-squeezed apple juice
1/2 tsp cinnamon
Dash of Celtic sea salt to taste

Strain flax seeds, raisins, and sesame seeds of any excess water. Mix together in a large bowl, adding in apple juice, cinnamon, and dash of salt. Spread out on teflex sheets, score, and dehydrate for 2 days or until done. These crackers should be dry and crunchy. Store covered in a cool dry place.

Pumpkin Sesame Seed Crackers

2 cups pumpkin seeds, soaked overnight
1 cup sesame seeds, soaked 4 hours
1/2 cup chopped onion
1 large red bell pepper
1 large zucchini or 2 smaller ones
1 1/2 cups chopped butternut squash or acorn squash
1 tsp sea salt
2–3 cloves garlic

Pumpkin seeds with all that wonderful zinc in them are so healthy for the skin, hair, and nails. They are especially healthy for the prostate, so any chance you can get to eat them, do. This cracker is hearty and filling and tastes very yummy.

Rinse seeds well and drain. Remove seeds from bell peppers and chop into pieces that will fit through the Champion juicer. Do the same for the squashes. With the blank in place, run the vegetables and seeds through the juice hopper, alternating so that the vegetables push the seeds through. If there is excess liquid from the vegetables after passing through the juicer, then carefully strain this off.

Mix thoroughly, adjusting the spices to your taste. Spread out on a teflex sheet and dehydrate 24–30 hours, making sure that both sides are dry and the cracker is nice and crunchy. Store in a cool dry place.

Vegetable Chips

These make great snacks with any of the dips or sauces.

Carrots
Yams
Zucchini
Turnips
Marinade

Any root vegetable will work, and you can experiment with this yourself. Slice these vegetables very thin using a mandolin or other kind of slicer. Slice them to maximize the surface area, i.e., diagonally. You can dehydrate as is or marinate these in your favorite marinade overnight, and then dehydrate until crispy.

Eggplant Marinara Crisps

1 eggplant
1 recipe Marinara Sauce

These cracker-type crisps are delicious, and you'd never guess that they are made from eggplant.

Peel eggplant and slice ¼ inch thick. Marinate overnight in the Marinara Sauce. Place on teflex sheets and dehydrate until crispy on one side, then flip them over to dehydrate on the other side. I don't know how to store these, as they get eaten so quickly.

148

Croutons

A crouton is a crunchy little addition that can be sprinkled on salads or used as a garnish for soups. They also make great snacks.

Sunflower Croutons

2 cups sunflower seeds,
soaked overnight

¼ cup olive oil

Nama Shoyu or Celtic sea salt to taste

1 tsp chili powder

1 Tbs Tomato Powder

1 tsp cumin

1 tsp onion powder

¼ tsp cayenne

Mix all the ingredients together, making sure that the seeds are well coated. Spread out on a teflex sheet and dehydrate for two days or until dry and crunchy. Store in a dry place, and they will last for months.

Variation: Marinate in Bragg's or Nama Shoyu to cover and dehydrate.

Curry Pumpkin Seed Croutons

2 cups pumpkin seeds,
soaked overnight

¼ cup olive oil

2 tsp kelp, Nama Shoyu,
or Celtic sea salt to taste

1 tsp garlic powder

1 tsp onion powder

1 tsp curry powder

1 tsp cumin

A wonderful source of zinc to nourish the hair, skin, nails, and prostate, these croutons make a great snack.

Mix all ingredients together and spread on a teflex sheet. Dehydrate until dry and crunchy, approximately two days. Store in a covered container in a cool dry place.

Almond Croutons

1 cup almonds, soaked overnight
1 cup Bragg's Liquid Aminos
or Nama Shoyu

Marinate almonds in Bragg's for 6 hours or longer. Strain and dehydrate until dry, about two days. These will last forever if you don't eat them all too quickly.

Spicy Cashew Croutons

1 cup cashew nuts, soaked overnight
2 Tbs honey or agave syrup
1/2 tsp chili powder
1/4 tsp cayenne pepper
Celtic sea salt to taste

Combine cashews with the rest of the ingredients and spread out on a teflex sheet. Dehydrate until crispy.

Spicy Pepitas

1 cup pumpkin seeds, soaked
overnight and rinsed
4 garlic cloves, pressed
2 tsp ground dried chile peppers
or cayenne to taste
Pinch of sea salt
1 tsp honey
Dash of lime juice

This is a Mexican-style pumpkin seed crouton with a bit of a zip to it. Try this recipe with different kinds of nuts or seeds.

Mix pumpkin seeds with garlic, ground chile pepper, sea salt, honey, and lime juice. Place on teflex sheets and dehydrate until crunchy.

Spicy Banana Chips

2 bananas sliced on the diagonal
2 Tbs light olive oil
Juice of 1 lime
1/2 tsp chili powder
1/2 tsp cinnamon

Mix chili powder, cinnamon, lime juice, and olive oil together and brush banana chips. Dehydrate on a teflex sheet for 16 hours, then turn over and dehydrate the other side.

Granolas

Raw Muesli

½ cup raw rolled oat groats, soaked in warm water 4 hours

½ cup raw rolled rye groats, soaked in warm water 4 hours

½ cup buckwheat groats, soaked overnight

¼ cup pumpkin seeds, soaked overnight

¼ cup sunflower seeds, soaked overnight

2 Tbs sesame seeds, soaked 4 hours

¼ cup walnuts and/or pecans, soaked 4 hours

¼ cup raisins, soaked 4 hours

This is a warm dish for those cool morning breakfasts. If you have digestive problems then I don't recommend this recipe, as the mixing of fruits with grains, or nut with grains, can sometimes be hard on the digestion.

Soak oat and rye groats in warm pure water for 4 hours. Drain well and place in medium-size bowl. Soak and drain all other ingredients and add to the groats. Feel free to add other dried fruits if you desire. If you do so then soak them first to soften. Mix well and serve with any nut milk.

This recipe can be heated, either in the dehydrator for ½ hour, or by slowly stirring it on the stove with the lowest heat possible. Make sure that the temperature does not go above 105 degrees. Makes 3 cups.

Grape Nutty Cereal

Granola

*2 cups flax seeds, soaked 2–4 hours
in 4 cups water*

1 cup sesame seeds, soaked 2 hours

1 cup pumpkin seeds, soaked 6 hours

1 cup almonds, soaked overnight

*1 cup sunflower seeds, soaked
overnight, rinsed, and cleaned*

*1 recipe unsweetened
Grape Nutty Cereal*

1 cup rolled oat groats

1 cup grated dried coconut

1 cup honey or agave syrup

1 Tbs vanilla

1 Tbs cinnamon

½ cup olive oil

2 tsp Celtic sea salt

Rinse and drain all soaked nuts and seeds and place in a large bowl. With the flax seed, simply strain off any excess liquid. There is no need to wash these seeds, as the gel around the seed is what will hold the rest of the ingredients together. Add the rolled oats, buckwheat, and coconut to the mixture. Add in the olive oil, honey, vanilla, cinnamon, and sea salt. Mix well then spread on the teflex sheets in the dehydrator (about one-half inch thick) and dehydrate until dry and crunchy. Break into small pieces and store in a large jar in a cool dry place.

Variation: Tropical Granola

After dehydrating the Basic Granola recipe, add in a mixture of dried tropical fruits such as raisins, dates, fig pieces, dried pineapple, or mango. Serve with Sesame or Almond Milk.

Grape Nutty Cereal

*3 cups raw buckwheat groats, soaked
overnight and sprouted for two days*

Nut or seed milk

Bananas

Raisins

Walnuts

This is a delicious crunchy cereal loaded with natural nutrients.

When your buckwheat grains have tiny little tails growing on them you know that you are ready to dehydrate.

If you like sweet cereal, mix thoroughly ¼–½ cup of agave syrup into your buckwheat. Spread evenly over a teflex sheet and dehydrate until dry and crunchy. Store in a covered container in a cool dry place.

Serve with Sesame or Almond Milk. You can also add chopped bananas or other fruit, along with raisins and walnuts, to make a hearty breakfast cereal.

For milks see the Nut & Seed Milks section.

Yogurt

"Yogurt" can be made from soaked macadamia nuts, blanched almonds, sunflower seeds, pine nuts, cashews, or combinations of these.

Simply use twice as much soaked seeds or nuts to water, blend well, and strain through a mesh seed bag or cheesecloth. Save pulp for another occasion. Let the milk sit out at room temperature 8–12 hours. Cover with a tea towel. The mixture will separate. Place in the fridge for another 8–12 hours to further solidify the creamy yogurt on the top. Scoop yogurt out carefully so as not to disturb the whey in the bottom of the container. Keeps up to five days in the fridge. Discard the whey or use as a base in other recipes.

Fruit Yogurts

Use any soft fleshy fruits. Mash or blend fruit and gently fold into the yogurt. Sweeten with honey or agave syrup if desired.

Quick & Easy Yogurt

If you're in a hurry and have coconuts lying around, this recipe makes a great quick yogurt. Try adding your favorite fruit to it.

1 medium young coconut
(should have rubbery meat inside)
1 lime
Agave syrup or honey to taste

Cut open coconut and save the water. Spoon coconut meat from the inside shell. Be careful not to scrape the brown inside membrane of the coconut. Place coconut meat and enough coconut water to cover the meat in the Vita-Mix. Add in lime juice and blend. Slowly add in agave syrup or honey to taste. If mixture is too thick then add in a little more coconut water, blending to achieve the consistency of yogurt. Chill and serve.

Basic Nut Creams/Sauces or Dips

To make any kind of cream, follow the recipe for the nut milks (see Nut & Seed Milks and Shakes) but use up to one half less water. Strain through a cheesecloth or fine-mesh sprout bag. Save the pulp for other dishes. The following recipe is a nice base for any cream sauce, cream soup, or dip that you may want to make. You can be versatile with this recipe, creating sauces and dips of different colors to complement the rest of your menu.

To make a green-colored sauce or dip, simply add parsley and/or basil to the basic recipe. For a yellow sauce, try adding a little turmeric, curry powder, and/or cumin. For a red sauce, try a little dehydrated Tomato Powder or Red Bell Pepper Powder (see Seasoning Powders). If you really want to get brave, try it with some beet juice or dehydrated Beet Powder. This makes an incredible purple sauce or dip. Just add enough of the vegetables to achieve your desired color and then spice it up to your taste.

Nut Cream or Sauce

1 cup blanched almonds, pine nuts,
cashews, or macadamia nuts,
soaked overnight
¼ cup lemon juice
1 tsp Celtic sea salt, Bragg's,
or Nama Shoyu to taste
2–3 cloves garlic
Jalapeño or cayenne to taste
Water for consistency

Blend all ingredients, adding enough water for desired consistency. Makes 1½ cups.

Sweet Nut Cream

1 cup almonds, pine nuts, cashews,
or macadamia nuts, soaked overnight
1 cup orange juice or coconut water
¼ cup agave syrup or honey to taste
1 tsp vanilla or vanilla bean

Blend all together in the Vita-Mix until smooth, adding more liquid if necessary. Makes 2 cups.

Coconut Cream

2–3 mature coconuts

A divinely rich, creamy sauce made with the best dietary oil on earth. (See *The Healing Miracles of Coconut Oil* in the Recommended Reading list.) This cream sauce makes a great base for soups and dressings.

Open the coconuts with a machete, removing and saving the water for later. Carefully remove the hard white coconut meat inside and cut into small chunks. Put through the Champion juicer with the screen attachment. A thick white cream will be extracted which you can use immediately or chill, if you desire a thicker consistency.

Please note that this recipe is an unsweetened version of Coconut Cream Frosting (see Frostings), which is a sweet, flavored sauce.

Quick Nut/Seed Cheese

To make a cheese, follow the recipe for the Nut Cream sauces above, but use less water so that the mixture is stiffer. Or you can choose to pour the sauce through a seed bag or cheesecloth and let sit overnight in the fridge with a bowl to catch the drips. The excess water will drain, and you will be left with your cheese. Store in an airtight container. This will keep for about 4 days in the fridge. Makes 1½ cups.

Macadamia Nut Cilantro Cheese

1½ cups macadamia nuts, soaked overnight

⅔ cup chopped cilantro

¼ cup lemon juice

¼ cup olive oil

2 cloves garlic

½ tsp paprika

Dash of cayenne or fresh ground black pepper

Celtic sea salt to taste

This is a quick and tasty nut cheese that makes a great spread on crackers or a filling for sushi.

Rinse nuts and place in the blender or food processor with all the rest of the ingredients. Blend or process until you have a thick cheesy texture. Add a little water if necessary. Keeps 5–7 days in the fridge. Makes 2 cups.

2 cups soaked sunflower seeds
1 cup soaked sesame seeds
3 cups rejuvelac or more

This recipe takes a little more time than the Basic Nut Cream recipe, but it is chock full of the friendly bacteria that our digestive systems need, so the extra effort is well worth it.

Soak seeds in separate bowls overnight. Make sure you have at least three times the amount of water to seeds for soaking. The sunflower seeds have thin translucent skins that will float on top of the water. Skim these off by filling the bowl with warm water, massaging the seeds carefully, then skimming the water off the seeds, being careful not to lose your seeds down the kitchen sink. Strain all the water off and place in the Vita-Mix. Rinse and drain the sesame seeds and place in the Vita-Mix along with the rejuvelac. Make sure there is enough rejuvelac to turn the blades comfortably without putting stress on the motor. Add more water if you need to. Blend until very smooth, like a smoothie consistency. Pour mixture into a large glass bowl and set on the counter for 4–6 hours. Cover with a tea towel. The mixture will separate into three layers. The top layer, which is about ¼ inch thick, will be a slight gray or brownish color. This is the oxidized layer and should be scraped off and discarded. The middle layer is the almost seed cheese layer: using a slotted spoon (one with holes), scoop the middle layer into a seed bag or strainer lined with cheesecloth. Squeeze remaining liquid out of the bag or cheesecloth, and hang in the fridge 8–10 hours, until the cheese has firmed up. Make sure you have a bowl underneath to catch the drips. (If you are using a cheesecloth, then fold over the edges and place the strainer over a bowl to catch the drips.) Store firmed cheese in an airtight container in the fridge. Seed cheese will usually last 4–5 days. The bottom layer is the whey, which I throw away or use in other recipes.

Variations:

Seasoned Seed Cheese

Simply blend in fresh herbs or vegetables, either by blending with the seeds and rejuvelac or adding after the seed cheese is made. Apply this theory to any of the following seed cheese recipes.

Pumpkin Seed Cheese

Follow the recipe for Basic Fermented Seed Cheese, but use pumpkin seeds instead of sunflower seeds.

Almond Seed Cheese

Follow the recipe for Basic Fermented Seed Cheese using blanched almonds instead of sunflower and sesame seeds.

Cashew Seed Cheese

Follow the recipe for Basic Fermented Seed Cheese using raw cashews (order from Rawfood.com or you are probably not going to be getting raw) instead of the sunflower and sesame seeds.

Macadamia Nut Seed Cheese

Follow the instructions for Basic Fermented Seed Cheese but use macadamia nuts only. This can be seasoned to your taste after it has been made.

Pine Nut Basil Seed Cheese

Follow the instruction for Basic Fermented Seed Cheese. Instead of sunflower seeds use 2 cups pine nuts (soaked for 6 hours) and 1 cup white sesame seeds. Add 1 cup chopped basil, 3 cloves of garlic, and blend with rejuvelac.

Curried Seed Cheese

Follow the instructions for Basic Fermented Seed Cheese but use blanched almonds instead of sunflower seeds. After seed cheese has been made, add in 1 Tbs Indian Spice Mix (see Seasoning Powders), Celtic sea salt, and pepper to taste.

Feta Cheese

1 cup soaked pine nuts
½ cup soaked cashew nuts
1½ cup rejuvelac

Blend nuts with rejuvelac until smooth and let ferment for 6 hours. Scoop off the top layer and spread out on a teflex sheet ¼ inch thick. (The top layer on pine nuts does not turn brown and oxidize like the other seeds.) Dehydrate 6 hours then flip over and dehydrate another 1–2 hours. Break up into small pieces and store in the fridge. Serve with Greek Salad.

Baked Goat Cheese

2 cups Almond Seed Cheese
Crumb Topping, see below

Make patties 1 inch thick and place on teflex sheet that has Crumb Topping sprinkled on it. Cover the top and sides of the patties with the crushed crumb topping and dehydrate until firm. Carefully turn over to dehydrate the other side. You can crush more crumbs on this side if desired.

Crumb Topping

Crush any kind of raw cracker in a food processor and use for this purpose.

Whipped "Butter"

1 avocado
1 Tbs flax oil
Pinch of sea salt

This makes a nice spread on the raw breads or crackers and has the omega essential fatty acids that we need.

Mash and blend avocado, olive oil, and sea salt together. Serve immediately.

Sour Cream #1

*1 cup soaked cashews,
macadamia nuts, or pine nuts*
¼–½ cup celery juice
½ cup peeled chopped cucumber
¼ cup chopped onion or shallots
1–2 Tbs lemon or lime juice
*¼ cup chopped garlic chives
(optional)*
1–2 cloves garlic
Celtic sea salt to taste

This rich sauce makes a nice addition to any Mexican dish or vegetable platter. If you like the taste to be more on the sour side, then just add a little more lemon or lime juice.

Place cucumber, celery, and lemon juice in blender and blend well. Add the remaining ingredients and blend until smooth or to achieve desired consistency. Makes 2 cups.

Sour Cream #2

*2 cups chopped mature
coconut meat*
2 Tbs lemon juice or lime juice

Make coconut cream by running the coconut chunks through the Champion juicer. Place in a bowl and chill until it firms up. Add lemon or lime juice and serve. Makes ⅔ cup.

Sour Cream #3

¼ cup pine nuts, soaked 6 hours
1 large avocado
2 Tbs lemon juice
Water (if necessary to blend)

Blend all together and chill.

Real Cheesy Sauce

1 cup soaked and blanched almonds
¼ cup soaked macadamia nuts
1 large red bell pepper, chopped
1 Tbs nutritional yeast flakes or ground-up flax seeds
1 clove garlic
½ tsp Celtic sea salt or 1 Tbs Nama Shoyu
Squeeze of lime or lemon to taste

After trying this you will never want to eat commercial cheese sauces again. This is delicious served as a dip, a sauce over vegetables, or as a spread on bread and crackers.

Soak almonds overnight and blanch. Soak macadamia nuts for 3 hours. Rinse nuts and place in the blender with the rest of the ingredients. Blend until smooth. Makes 2 cups.

Cheese Patties

3 cups corn kernels cut from the cob
¼ cup flax meal (ground flax seeds)
½ cup fresh-squeezed carrot juice
1 Tbs nutritional yeast flakes
1 tsp Celtic sea salt
1 Tbs lime juice
1 tsp jalapeño
2 cloves garlic
1 tsp minced ginger
¼ tsp curry
¼ tsp cumin
¼ tsp turmeric

These are delicious served with a garden burger, or if made very thin can be used as a taco shell or burrito skin.

Make flax meal by soaking, dehydrating, and grinding flax seeds in a coffee grinder until mealy. Place all other ingredients in blender and blend until smooth. Add flax meal last.

Using a serving spoon, spoon batter onto dehydrator sheets in small circles about 4 inches in diameter and ¼ inch thick. Dehydrate for six hours at 105 degrees, turning to dry the other side. You don't want these to be dried like a cracker, but instead a little soft and chewy. Makes approximately 24 slices of cheese.

Pine Nut Parmesan Cheese

1 cup pine nuts, soaked 6–8 hours

Rinse and dehydrate until dry and crunchy. Place in food processor and grind up fine. If too moist after grinding, place on teflex sheet again and dehydrate for another 24 hours. Keep refrigerated. Makes 1 cup.

Variation: Crumble up one half of a cauliflower until mealy, using a very fine grater. Mix with ½ cup ground dehydrated pine nuts. This makes a great garnish for pasta dishes.

Marinades
and Dressings

To marinate vegetables you can use onions, mushrooms, zucchini, bell peppers, or thinly shaved strips of carrots or squash. I marinate vegetables in just enough marinade to cover. I like to marinate overnight, but six hours is usually sufficient to soften. You can also use any of the vinaigrette dressings in this book, Bragg's Liquid Aminos, or the popular Simple Marinade (see below).

Simple Marinade

½ cup olive oil
¼ cup lemon juice
½ cup water
1-inch piece of ginger, grated
2 cloves garlic, minced
1 Tbs Nama Shoyu

This marinade is versatile and can be used to marinate a variety of vegetables. I like to use this marinade for softening mushrooms, onions, bell peppers, zucchini, broccoli, cauliflower, etc. Marinating vegetables can help with digestive problems, especially with the cruciferous vegetables such as broccoli and cauliflower.

Blend all together. This will keep for two weeks in the fridge.

Sesame Ginger Marinade

⅓ cup Bragg's or Nama Shoyu
3 Tbs sesame seed oil
1 Tbs sesame seeds, ground
1 Tbs sesame seeds, whole
(black sesame seeds look great)
2 green onions, minced
2 Tbs honey
2 tsp grated ginger root
4 cloves garlic, minced or grated
½ tsp dried red pepper (hot)

Mix all ingredients together and keep refrigerated.

Dressings

Just about any soup or sauce recipe in this book can be used as a dressing after being blended to a smooth consistency.

Please note that when making salad dressings or any recipe that needs olive oil, it's always best to use the cold-pressed extra-virgin olive oil, or better still, the stone-ground olive oil from Rawfood.com (see Resources list).

Dressings are best used within three days and must be refrigerated. All oils should be kept in the fridge after opening.

Herbed Olive Oil

1 cup olive oil
1/4 cup fresh oregano
1/4 cup fresh basil
1/4 cup fresh rosemary
1/4 cup fresh tarragon leaves

This is a seasoned olive oil with many uses. I like to drizzle it over soups, use in dressings, or as a preservative for dried tomatoes.

Blend oil with herbs in the Vita-Mix until smooth. Place in a glass jar and refrigerate for 24 hours. You can strain oil or use as is. Keep refrigerated.

Variation: Basil Olive Oil

Follow instructions above but use 1 cup chopped basil with the oil.

Roasted Bell Pepper Olive Oil

1 large red bell pepper, cut into chunks
1 cup extra-virgin olive oil
1/4 habanero chile pepper

Dehydrate bell peppers until soft and chewy. Do not dry completely. Blend peppers with olive oil and let sit for two days in the fridge. Strain and keep refrigerated. Use as needed.

Orange Tahini Dressing

½ cup fresh-squeezed orange juice

¼ cup extra-virgin olive oil

2 Tbs flax oil

2 Tbs sesame oil

2 Tbs raw tahini

2 cloves garlic

1 Tbs ginger

¼ cup chopped shallots

1–2 Tbs agave syrup or honey

½ tsp cumin

2 Tbs Nama Shoyu
or Celtic sea salt to taste

¼ tsp jalapeño or pinch of cayenne

Put all ingredients into the blender or Vita-Mix and blend until smooth. Makes about 1½ cups.

Creamy Tahini Dressing

1 cup pure water
or young coconut water

¾ cup raw sesame tahini

¼ cup Nama Shoyu
or Celtic Sea salt to taste

½ cup fresh chopped parsley,
dill, or basil

½ cup fresh lemon juice

¼ cup chopped onions

1 Tbs minced ginger

3 cloves garlic

1-2 tsp cumin

¼ tsp cayenne or jalapeño pepper

This Asian-type dressing is a smooth, creamy, high-calcium recipe. It makes a nice sauce for dipping vegetables or as a dressing over any salad.

Blend all ingredients until smooth, adding more water if desired. Serve chilled.

Avocado Tomatillo Ginger Dressing

1 cucumber, chopped

1/4 cup extra-virgin olive oil (optional)

1 avocado

3 tomatillos

1 clove garlic

1/2 tsp dill seed

1 1/2 tsp minced ginger

This versatile dressing is made with tomatillos, which look like little green tomatoes wrapped up in their own individual jackets. These green leaves protecting the fruit need to be peeled off before using. Try this dressing made with different herbs for variety. This is a simple dressing. If you do not have tomatillos, then substitute with 2 Tbs lemon juice.

Blend cucumber to create a liquid base, then add all the other ingredients. You can vary this recipe by adding different fresh herbs such as basil, dill, or parsley.

Avocado Tomatillo Ginger Dressing

Vinaigrettes

These are very simple dressings that can be blended to a smooth consistency. Traditionally these are made with vinegars, but vinegar tends to have an acidic response in the body. The only vinegar recommended for a raw-foods lifestyle is organic raw apple cider vinegar. If you choose not to use vinegar, then substitute with lemon or lime juice.

Herbed Vinaigrette

1 cup extra-virgin olive oil

½ cup water

¼ cup apple cider vinegar or lemon juice

¼ cup flax seed oil

1 Tbs honey

1 tsp mustard seed, ground (optional)

½ tsp Celtic sea salt

2 cloves garlic

½ tsp minced ginger

¼ tsp jalapeño

1 Tbs mixed dried herbs (parsley, basil, dill)

This is one of my favorite recipes, to which I will sometimes add a little mustard seed ground up. I also like to use fresh herbs when I can, so I invite you to try this recipe both ways.

Blend all ingredients together. Will last 7–10 days refrigerated. Makes 2 cups.

Mustard Dill Vinaigrette

¼ cup apple cider vinegar

3 Tbs lemon juice

¼ cup olive oil

1 Tbs mustard seed

1 Tbs honey

3 Tbs fresh dill weed, chopped

2 Tbs minced green onions

Celtic sea salt or Bragg's to taste

Blend all ingredients, adding the salt last. Salt to taste and serve. Makes 1 cup.

Cranberry Vinaigrette

¼ cup dried cranberries, soaked in
¾ cup water for 2 hours
½ cup extra-virgin olive oil
¼ cup raw apple cider vinegar
2 Tbs lemon juice
2 cloves garlic
1 Tbs honey
1 tsp minced ginger
¼–½ tsp Celtic sea salt
or Bragg's to taste
Additional water if necessary

This vinaigrette has a tangy taste and is a nice variation to the basic Herbed Vinaigrette.

Place all ingredients in the Vita-Mix and blend until smooth. Add more water if necessary. Keeps ten days refrigerated. Makes 1⅓ cups.

Strawberry Vinaigrette

½ cup extra-virgin olive oil
¼ cup apple cider vinegar
or lemon juice
¼ cup water
6 large strawberries
1–2 cloves garlic
1 tsp honey

Strawberries are known for their pain-relieving qualities; they also are a powerful anti-aging food. Combined with the following ingredients, strawberries make one of the most delicious dressings.

Place all ingredients in the Vita-Mix and blend until smooth. Add more water if necessary. Makes 1⅓ cups.
Variation: Any other berry in season can be substituted in this recipe, so be creative.

Raspberry Vinaigrette

¼ cup fresh raspberries
¼ cup olive oil
¼ cup apple cider vinegar
1 tsp mustard seed
2 Tbs honey
1 clove garlic
Celtic sea salt to taste
Pinch of cayenne
or ground black peppercorns

Blend all ingredients, salt to taste, and serve. Makes approximately ⅔ cup.

Orange Vinaigrette

½ cup fresh-squeezed orange juice
¼ cup apple cider vinegar
¼ cup extra-virgin olive oil
1 Tbs honey
1–2 cloves garlic
1 tsp ginger
Celtic sea salt, Bragg's,
or Nama Shoyu to taste
Pinch of cayenne or jalapeño pepper

This dressing is loaded with vitamin C. Combined with the other ingredients, it helps to flush the liver out. It's quite tasty too.

Blend all ingredients and serve. Makes 1 cup.

Pink Grapefruit Vinaigrette

½ cup pink grapefruit juice
½ cup pink grapefruit segments
⅓ cup light olive oil
¼ cup apple cider vinegar
1 Tbs honey
1–2 garlic cloves
1 tsp minced ginger (optional)
Celtic sea salt to taste

The benefits of this dressing are similar to the Orange Vinaigrette, with the added bonus of being a fat burner.

Cut out grapefruit segments with a sharp knife. Place all ingredients in a Vita-Mix and blend until smooth.

Lemon Vinaigrette

½ cup stoned-ground extra-virgin olive oil (available from Rawfood.com)
½ cup lemon juice
½–1 tsp Celtic sea salt, Nama Shoyu, or Bragg's

This recipe has a simple but flavorful taste. It is the type of olive oil here that makes the difference. Stone-ground olive oil is the highest-quality olive oil, as there is no heat generated in the process of extraction. The flavor is rich and earthy and adds to any recipe that you use it in.

Blend all ingredients. Makes 1 cup.

Papaya Seed Dressing

½ cup olive oil

¼ cup apple cider vinegar

¼–½ cup water

1 cup chopped papaya

2–3 Tbs papaya seeds

2 garlic cloves

½ tsp minced ginger

Juice from one lemon

1 Tbs honey

Celtic sea salt or Bragg's to taste

Digestive enzymes anyone? Well, here you have it— an abundance of enzymes and antioxidants.

Blend all ingredients in Vita-Mix until the mixture had a smooth consistency. Makes 2½ cups.

Persimmon Dressing

½ cup extra-virgin olive oil

¼ cup apple cider vinegar or lemon juice

¼ cup water

1 persimmon

1–2 cloves garlic

1 Tbs Bragg's

Honey to taste (optional)

Ummmm, try this one on your guests—you'll be a hit!

Blend all together in the Vita-Mix until smooth and serve. Makes 1½ cups.

Thousand Island

½ cup blanched almonds or sunflower seeds

1 cup pure water

1 cup olive oil

1 tsp ground mustard seed

2 Tbs minced soaked sun-dried tomatoes or Tomato Powder

1 Tbs minced black sun-dried olives (order from Rawfood.com)

2 Tbs minced cucumber

1 Tbs fresh dill

1 Tbs lime juice

½–1 tsp honey (optional)

1 tsp Celtic sea salt

½ tsp paprika

A traditional dressing with a slightly different twist.

Blend almonds with water, slowly adding in olive oil. If you desire, you can use a combination of oils such as olive, flax, sesame, or sunflower. Make olive oil the most prominent if you do this. The combination gives you a good spectrum of essential fatty acids. Add in mustard powder or ground mustard seed, soaked dried tomatoes, dill, lime juice, honey, salt and paprika. Blend until thick and smooth. Add in minced olives and cucumber. Makes 2¾ cups. Keeps approximately 4 days refrigerated.

Cranberry Durian Cream

½ cup cranberries

1 cup durian

½ cup water

½ cup olive oil

2 Tbs lemon juice

1 clove garlic

1 tsp minced ginger

Sea salt or Bragg's to taste

The best of Asian beauty foods, durian in this concoction provides the body with elements of exotic East Asia.

Scoop out durian flesh from durian pod and add to the Vita-Mix. Add in remaining ingredients. Blend and serve. Makes 2½ cups.

Salsas

A popular side dish for any Mexican recipe. Salsa can be varied in many ways, using different fruits or vegetables and combining them with the flavors of Mexico.

Tomato Salsa

1½ cups chopped tomatoes
½ cup minced red onion
1 Tbs minced scallions
2 Tbs minced red bell pepper
½ cup chopped cilantro
1 Tbs lime juice or lemon juice
¼ cup olive oil
1 tsp Celic sea salt
½ tsp minced Serrano chiles
½ tsp cumin
1 Tbs Tomato Powder (optional)

Place one half of the ingredients into the blender and blend on low speed until thoroughly mixed. Mix in remaining ingredients, giving the salsa a chunky texture. Makes 2 cups.

Variation: To add more color and make this more festive, try adding some corn cut from the cob. Add about ½ cup of corn kernels. If the recipe is too thick, you can blend up some tomatoes and add them in, adjusting the seasonings if necessary.

Creamy Cilantro Salsa

½ cup pine nuts, soaked overnight
⅔ cup water
½ cup chopped cilantro
2 minced tomatillos
¼ cup minced red onions
2 cloves minced garlic
1 tsp minced jalapeño
Sea salt or Bragg's to taste

Blend nuts and fresh water in the Vita-Mix to make a creamy base. Place in a bowl and mix in remaining ingredients. Makes 2½ cups.

Tomatillo Salsa

Mango Jicama Salsa

1 large mango, peeled and diced

1 cup peeled and diced jicama

1/4 cup diced red onion

1 Tbs fresh mint, minced

1 Tbs lime juice

*1/2 tsp minced jalapeño
or Serrano chile peppers*

Celtic sea salt to taste

In a bowl combine mango, jicama, onion, mint, lime juice, and salt. Discard seeds from pepper. Mince pepper and add to mixture. Makes 2 cups.

Tomatillo Salsa

8 tomatillos, minced

1/2 onion, minced

2–3 cloves garlic, minced

2/3 cup cilantro

2 Tbs lemon or lime juice

2 Tbs olive oil

*1 tsp Mexican Seasoning Mix
(see Seasoning Powders)*

dash of Celtic sea salt

Combine all ingredients and serve.

Papaya Salsa

½ Mexican papaya or 1 whole regular Hawaiian papaya, minced

½ medium sweet onion, minced

1 cup cilantro or 1 cup basil, minced

1 red bell pepper, minced

2 tomatoes, diced

3 garlic cloves, minced

1-inch piece of ginger, minced or grated fine

¼–½ cup lemon juice

¼–½ tsp jalapeño pepper, minced

1 tsp chili powder

1 tsp cumin

1–2 Tbs olive oil

This is one of my favorite salsas for serving with nut loafs, or enjoying with Mexican food, or as a condiment with sushi rolls.

Combine all ingredients together. If you want it saucier, then put ⅓ of the ingredients into the blender and pulse chop, then add back to other ingredients. Makes about 5 cups and will last in the fridge for about four days. This makes a delicious garnish with many dishes, such as nori rolls and burgers.

Variation: Persimmon Salsa

See Papaya Salsa. Instead of using papaya, make with 3 cups diced and peeled persimmons.

Tropical Salsa

½ cup diced pineapple

½ cup diced mango

½ cup diced papaya

⅓ cup diced red onion

½ cup diced tomatoes

½ cup diced red bell peppers

½ cup chopped cilantro

3 cloves minced garlic

1 tsp minced ginger

¼ cup lemon or lime juice

3 Tbs olive oil

1–2 tsp jalapeño, minced

1–2 tsp Celtic sea salt or Bragg's to taste

Mix all ingredients and serve. Makes 3½ cups.

Mango Salsa

1½ cups diced firm ripe mango
⅓ cup minced red onion
⅓ cup minced cilantro
½ tsp chili powder
Pinch of sea salt
Squeeze of lime juice

Mix all ingredients together. Makes 2 cups.

Mango Cherry Salsa

1 cup cherries (use a cherry that is a bit on the sour side)
1 cup chopped mango
¼ cup chopped green onions
3 Tbs chopped cilantro
1 Tbs lemon or lime juice
2 Tbs olive oil
1–2 tsp jalapeño, seeded and minced
Celtic sea salt to taste

Combine all ingredients in a bowl and serve.

Jicama Salsa

1 jicama, peeled and diced
1 red onion, minced
2 oranges, peeled and segmented
1½ cup diced cucumber with seeds removed
1 red Serrano chile, minced
2 Tbs minced cilantro
Juice from 1 lime
Avocado (optional)

Mix all ingredients and chill. Garnish with diced avocado and a squeeze of lime.

Jicama Salsa

Sauces and Dips

Sauces and dips make a wonderful accompaniment to any meal. Use them as a garnish or to add a little extra flavor and richness.

I like to use coconut water in my recipes as much as possible, as this truly is nature's purest water. The clear water is one of the highest sources of electrolytes found in nature, and the young spoon meat is a restorative for oxidative tissue damage and male sexual fluids.

Note that in many of the following recipes you will see the term "blanching" used. This usually refers to almonds in this book and is a process to remove the skins.

To blanch almonds, boil some water and let sit for 1 minute, then quickly add the almonds and let sit for 15 seconds. Remove immediately and place in ice-cold water. Let sit for about five minutes then squeeze the almonds between your fingers to release their skins.

Red Bell Pepper Sauce

1 large red bell pepper

½ cup water

½ cup soaked sunflower seeds, cashews, or macadamia nuts

¼ cup chopped red onion

1–2 Tbs lemon juice

¼ tsp ginger, minced

Dash of cayenne pepper

Celtic sea salt to taste

1 Tbs olive oil (optional)

This is a creamy pink sauce full of vitamin C and essential fatty acids. It is delicious as a vegetable dip or served as a sauce served over a bed of mixed sprouts.

Blend all ingredients together in the Vita-Mix and serve. You can make this recipe hotter by adding more cayenne or jalapeño. Makes 2 cups.

Tomatillo Cream Sauce

*1 recipe Cashew Cream Sauce
(see Creams, Yogurts,
and Cheeses section)*
12–14 tomatillos
*1–2 tsp minced Serrano chiles
or to taste*
2–3 garlic cloves
¼ cup olive oil
Celtic sea salt to taste
*Coconut water from
a young coconut*

A Mexican favorite, tomatillos are full of vitamin C. This sauce can be served with any Mexican dish or simply as a dip for vegetables. If making a dip, use less liquid in the recipe.

Combine all ingredients in the Vita-Mix, adding enough coconut water to achieve the right consistency. Makes 2 cups. Serve with Enchiladas or Chiles Rellenos.

Guajillo Chile Sauce

2 bell peppers
3 tomatoes
2 Ancho chiles
2 Guajillo chiles
3 garlic cloves
2 Tbs Sun-Dried Tomato Paste
1¼ cups coconut water
*1 tsp Mixed Italian Seasoning
(see Seasoning Powders); could
substitute standard poultry seasoning*
1 tsp dried oregano
1 tsp honey

This Mexican favorite is a rich chile sauce that makes a nice accompaniment to raw tacos, burritos, or enchiladas.

Soak chiles in warm water for half an hour. Remove seeds and blend with all other ingredients. Serve with Enchiladas, Tacos, or Chiles Rellenos.

Variation: Chipotle Sauce

Make as above but use chipotle chiles instead of Guajillo chiles.

Enchilada Sauce

6–8 tomatoes

1/4 cup Tomato Powder
(see Seasoning Powders) or 1/2 cup
Sun-Dried Tomatoes in Olive Oil
(see Side Dishes)

2 Tbs chili powder

2 garlic cloves

1/2 tsp sea salt

1 tsp cumin

Dash of cayenne or minced jalapeño

Water

This sauce makes a nice accompaniment for the Enchiladas entrée.

Blend all ingredients until smooth in consistency. Add a little water if too thick. Keep chilled. Makes 3 cups.

Curry Sauce

1/2 cup pine nuts, soaked 4–6 hours

1/2 cup cashews, soaked 4–6 hours

1 1/2 cups coconut water

2 limes, juiced

2–3 garlic cloves

2 tsp Indian Spice Mix

1 Tbs Bragg's or Celtic sea salt
to taste

1 tsp minced ginger

Blend all ingredients in the Vita-Mix until smooth and creamy.

Variation: Quick Curry Sauce

1/2 cup macadamia nut butter or cashew butter (you can also make the nut creams—see Yogurts, Creams, and Cheeses section)

1/4 cup olive oil

2–3 tsp Indian Spice Mix (see Seasoning Powders)

1 Tbs Bragg's or Nama Shoyu

1 1/2 cups coconut water

Blend all ingredients in the blender and serve over vegetable mixture. Serves 4.

Creamy Almond Curry Sauce

1 cup almonds, soaked overnight

1½ cup carrot juice

1 tsp curry powder

1 Tbs lemon juice

Celtic sea salt, Nama Shoyu,
or Bragg's

Dash of Seasoning Blend
(see Seasoning Powders)

This sauce with it rich nutty flavor is delicious served with the Pink Salmon Loaf entrée. If you want a smoother sauce, then blanch the almonds.

Blend all ingredients in the Vita-Mix. You can make this sauce or dressing thicker by adding more almonds. Makes 2 cups.

Marinara Sauce

4–6 tomatoes, chopped

½ large red bell pepper, chopped

¼ cup sun-dried tomatoes,
soaked 4 hours

¼ cup minced onion

⅓ cup olive oil

4 cloves garlic

½ tsp jalapeño, seeds removed,
or ⅛ tsp cayenne pepper

⅓ cup basil leaves

¼ cup fresh oregano

1 tsp Celtic sea salt

1 tsp minced ginger

An Italian staple for good reason, this sauce is delicious served with raw linguine or angel hair pasta. You can make the pasta with the Saladacco (see Food Preparation Basics). This recipe makes a good base sauce for Pizza, Lasagna, or Pasta Marinara.

Blend all ingredients until smooth and serve immediately. This sauce will thicken rapidly with time, so be aware. Makes 4 cups.

Pesto

This versatile food is synonymous with its Italian heritage. It makes a great dipping sauce for crackers, breads, or cut vegetables. I have used it on pizzas instead of cheese, and of course the all-too-familiar pasta dishes.

Basic Pesto

2 cups fresh basil leaves
2 cups fresh parsley
Lots of garlic to taste (I use about 4 cloves)
1½ cups pine nuts, soaked 6 hours or overnight
1 avocado
¼ cup olive oil
Pinch of fresh ginger
Jalapeño to taste (start with ⅛ tsp and add from there)
¼ cup lemon juice
1½ tsp Celtic sea salt, dulse, or kelp

Blend all ingredients until smooth. Serves 4–6. This sauce will keep for about 5 days chilled. If the top oxidizes, just scrape off a thin layer before serving.

Cilantro Pumpkin Seed Pesto

2 cups cilantro, firmly packed

1 cup basil

1 cup pumpkin seeds, soaked overnight, or 4 Tbs pumpkin seed butter

¼ cup pine nuts, soaked 4–6 hours

½ avocado

1 tsp Celtic sea salt

2 cloves garlic

1 Tbs minced garlic

¼ tsp cayenne pepper or 1 tsp minced jalapeño

¼ cup olive oil

¼ cup lemon or lime juice

I have made this recipe without pine nuts and also without olive oil. It's just as delicious. I've made it exclusively with cilantro, and that too is wonderful. Play around with this and try different nuts. Soaked sunflower seeds are good, as are walnuts.

Blend all ingredients until smooth. Makes 2 cups.

Spinach Pesto

Made the same as Cilantro Pumpkin Seed Pesto (above) but using spinach instead of cilantro. The rest of the ingredients can stay the same.

Sun-Dried Tomato Pesto

1 cup pine nuts

¾ cup sun-dried tomatoes, soaked for 3 hours

3 Tbs lemon juice

½ cup olive oil

4 cloves garlic

2 tablespoons minced fresh basil

1 tablespoon minced fresh oregano

Jalapeño to taste or pinch of cayenne

¼ tsp minced ginger

1 tsp Celtic sea salt

Squeeze water from tomatoes and save. Place tomatoes and all other ingredients in the Vita-Mix and blend until smooth. Add a little of the saved water, if necessary, to achieve the right consistency. You want the mixture to be able to turn over in the blender or Vita-Mix. Keeps for one week refrigerated. Makes 2 cups.

Teriyaki Sauce

½ cup *Nama Shoyu*

¼ cup *honey*

¼ *avocado*

2 tsp *minced ginger*

1 tsp *garlic powder*

1 tsp *onion powder*

1 tsp *minced galanga root*

Blend and serve. Makes ¾ cup.

Sweet & Sour Sauce

4 *Medjool dates, soaked 2 hours*

2 tsp *mustard seeds, ground fine*

1–2 tsp *apple cider vinegar*

2 *lemons, squeezed*

2 tsp *minced ginger*

2 Tbs *Nama Shoyu or Bragg's*

2 Tbs *olive oil*

¼ cup *fresh-squeezed orange juice or papaya juice*

¼ tsp *jalapeño (optional for hot and spicy)*

This sauce is wonderful served with the Vegetarian Spring Rolls or Stuffed Cabbage Rolls. I also like to have it as a side dish for Sushi.

Blend all ingredients and serve. Makes approximately 1 cup.

Beet Relish

1 large beet, grated
½ sweet onion, minced
½ cup olive oil
1 tsp minced ginger
1 clove garlic, minced
1½ Tbs lemon juice
Jalapeño, minced, to taste
Celtic sea salt, Bragg's, or Nama Shoyu to taste

Mix all ingredients and place in a glass jar. Will keep for seven days in the fridge.
Variation: You can make a Carrot Relish by substituting carrots for the beets, or better yet, try a combination relish. Makes 1½ cups.

Cranberry Orange Persimmon Relish

A wonderful Thanksgiving garnish to give thanks for, not push to the side of your plate.

2 cups cranberries
½–1 cup dates, soaked
2 persimmons, peeled and chopped
1 orange, peeled and seeded
Orange juice as needed

Add all the ingredients to the Vita-Mix or food processor with the S blade on it, using just enough orange juice to make a thick sauce. If you want a sweeter sauce, add more dates. Makes 2 cups.

"Peanut" Sauce

½ cup raw almond butter

¼ cup water

1 Tbs Nama Shoyu
or Bragg's Liquid Aminos

2 Tbs agave syrup or honey

1 Tbs minced garlic

1 Tbs minced ginger

2 Tbs lemon or lime juice

Jalapeño, habanero,
or hot Thai chile pepper to taste

This satisfying sauce is made with almonds instead of peanuts, because peanuts are very hard to digest, and most of them carry an aflatoxin (fungus) on them that is considered carcinogenic. Peanut butter is not used for the same reason. Almonds, however, provide a wonderful source of protein, calcium, and manganese, which transmutes into iron in the body as needed. This sauce is delicious served with Pad Thai Noodles, Vietnamese Spring Rolls, or any of the wraps.

Blend all ingredients until smooth, adding more water if necessary. Makes 1 cup.

Bar-B-Q Sauce

1 cup chopped tomatoes

¼ cup Tomato Powder
(see Seasoning Powders) or ½ cup
Sun-Dried Tomatoes in Olive Oil
(see Side Dishes)

⅛ tsp cayenne or ½ tsp jalapeño

3–4 Medjool dates, pitted
and soaked 2 hours

1 tsp Celtic sea salt

½ tsp ginger and garlic

¼ cup olive oil

2 tsp lemon juice or to taste

This is a delicious condiment that you can serve on a nut loaf or garden burger.

Blend all ingredients until smooth. Add a little water if too thick. Makes 1½ cups.

Cucumber Dill Sauce

1 cup cashews, soaked 4 hours

2 cloves garlic

2 large cucumbers, peeled and chopped

¼ cup fresh dill, minced

1–2 lemons, squeezed

1 tsp Celtic sea salt or 1 Tbs Nama Shoyu

Dash of cayenne or 1 tsp minced jalapeño

Not only is this a delicious sauce, it's so healthy for you. This recipe feeds the skin and helps to rebuild the kidneys. Try to use the real raw organic cashews from Rawfood.com (see Resources list).

Blend all ingredients in a food processor and chill for two hours before serving. Makes 1½ cups.

Mayonnaise

1 cup sunflower, cashew, or macadamia nuts (soaked for 4 hours)

1 avocado

½ cup chopped celery

¼ cup chopped tomatoes

¼ cup lemon juice

2 green onions

2 cloves garlic

2 Tbs minced fresh parsley

2 Tbs dulse or 1 tsp Celtic sea salt

Dash of cayenne or minced jalapeño

This makes a great spread for raw breads and also serves as a dressing with salads. It is full of all the healthy raw fats that our bodies need and provides a good source of enzymes and protein.

Blend all ingredients and chill. If too thick add a little water or coco water, or blend in some peeled cucumber. This recipe will stay fresh chilled for 3 days.

Hummus

2 cups sprouted chick peas
½ cup raw sesame tahini
2–3 lemons, juiced,
or ⅓ cup fresh-squeezed orange juice
2 Tbs olive oil
½ cup parsley, chopped
½ tsp cumin
2–3 cloves garlic
½ tsp minced jalapeño
Nama Shoyu or Celtic sea salt to taste

This Middle Eastern spread, made from sesame seeds (tahini), is delicious on crackers, breads, or used as part of the filling for Stuffed Portobello Mushrooms. Sesame seeds are one of the better food sources of calcium.

Blend all ingredients in the Vita-Mix until smooth. Add a tiny bit of water if too thick or a little more olive oil. Makes 2½ cups.

Variation: Carrot Hummus

Omit the parsley and run 2 peeled carrots through the Champion juicer, with blank attachment.

Nutty Hummus

1 cup almonds, soaked overnight
and then blanched
1 cup whole raw cashews,
soaked overnight
½ cup extra virgin olive oil
½ cup lemon or lime juice
1 Tbs garlic
¼ cup chopped onion
¼ cup water
1–2 tsp Celtic sea salt or to taste
2 Tbs minced parsley
Minced jalapeño to taste
Extra olive oil for garnish

Some folks have a difficult time digesting the chick peas normally used to make hummus, so this recipe provides a nice alternative.

Rinse and drain nuts. Using a food processor with the S blade in it or your Vita-Mix, blend all ingredients until a smooth consistency is achieved. Serve with additional olive oil drizzled on top. Makes approximately 4 cups.

Cranberry Sauce

4 cups fresh cranberries

2 oranges, peeled and seeded

2 apples, peeled and cored

1 cup pitted honey dates,
soaked 1 hour

Pure water if needed

Another nice addition to any Thanksgiving dinner. It is chock full of enzymes and vitamin C, and tastes so much better than its cooked counterpart.

Place all ingredients in the Vita-Mix or blender and blend until desired consistency is achieved. Use a little water if needed. If you want your sauce sweeter, add more dates and blend together with the rest of the mixture. Makes 3 cups.

Mushroom Sauce/Gravy

1 cup blanched almonds

1–2 cups young coconut water
or pure water

4½ cups shiitake mushrooms
(reserve ½ cup)

2–3 cloves garlic

Celtic sea salt or Nama Shoyu to taste

Blend almonds with 1 cup water until rich and creamy. Add in 4 cups mushrooms, garlic, sea salt, and remaining water. Blend until smooth. Chop the remaining mushrooms and stir into the gravy. Makes 3 cups.

Cauliflower Dip

1 large head cauliflower

½ cup basil leaves, loosely packed

1 avocado

6 cloves garlic

1 tsp ginger

1–2 limes, squeezed

½ tsp Celtic sea salt

Cauliflower is one of the cruciferous vegetables, known for their cancer prevention qualities. They are also high in fiber, along with many other nutrients and enzymes. Combined with the rest of these ingredients, this dip is not only very nutritious but delicious too.

Blend all ingredients to smooth consistency and serve. Makes 1½–2 cups dip.

Molé Sauce

2 red bell peppers, juiced

2 tomatoes

1 Ancho chile, seeded
and soaked 4 hours

1 Chipotle chile, seeded
and soaked 4 hours

1 tsp minced cilantro

3 Tbs minced onion

1 tsp mustard seed, ground
(optional)

1 tsp minced ginger

2 cloves garlic

2 Tbs almond butter

1/2 cup pitted prunes, soaked 2 hours

1/4 cup raisins, soaked 2 hours

2–3 Tbs unsweetened cacao powder

1 tsp chili powder or fresh chiles

Dash of cumin

1 tsp oregano

1 1/2 tsp of cinnamon, cardamom,
and cloves

Celtic sea salt to taste

This traditional Mexican sauce takes most of the day to make in the old way, and has many secret ingredients. This is a much simpler version, delicious served over Chiles Rellenos or Enchiladas.

Drain and rinse chiles and put in the Vita-Mix. Add remaining ingredients and blend well. Chill before serving, as it will help to thicken it further. Makes 1 1/2 cups.

Tamarind Sauce

1/4 cup Tamarind Puree (see below)

3 Tbs honey or agave syrup

2 Tbs olive oil

2 tsp minced Serrano chile
or jalapeño

1/2 tsp Celtic sea salt

1 Tbs minced garlic

1 1/2 tsp minced ginger

1/4 cup Nama Shoyu or Bragg's

Tamarind is a pod fruit with fleshy brown seeds. It is used extensively in Asian countries to flavor dishes, adding a unique taste.

Blend all ingredients in the Vita-Mix or blender until you have a smooth consistency. Serve with Pad Thai Noodles or Green Papaya Salad. Makes 2/3 cup.

Tamarind Puree

Take the fleshy tamarind seeds out of the tamarind shell and soak in water for 1–2 hours. Press seeds into a mesh sieve with the back of a large spoon or spatula. Scrape off the tamarind puree.

Variation: Tamarind Juice

Add water to the puree and honey to taste. This is a very popular drink in Mexico and Asia, noted for its laxative effect.

Sun-Dried Tomato Sauce/Paste

½ cup dried tomatoes, soaked,
or Tomato Powder
½ cup onions, chopped
1–2 cloves garlic
1 Tbs lime or lemon juice
¼ cup olive oil
1 Medjool date, soaked
¼ cup sun-dried olives (optional)
Celtic sea salt to taste

This is a good substitute for ketchup, or the ingredient to reach for if you want a real strong tomato flavor in a recipe. This is great served on top of Stuffed Cabbage Rolls or the mock meat loaves.

Place ingredients in the Vita-Mix and blend into a thick sauce, adding more water if necessary to acquire the right consistency. Use the soaking water for this. If making a paste, keep it thick. Makes 1⅓ cups.

Sunflower Beet Sauce

1 cup sunflower seeds, soaked overnight
½–1 beet
1–2 Tbs lemon or lime juice
2 cloves garlic
¼ tsp minced ginger
Celtic sea salt, Nama Shoyu,
or Bragg's to taste
Touch of honey to taste (optional)
Water for consistency

You won't believe the color of this sauce. It's amazing and so good. It makes a nice addition to the broccoli or spinach quiche.

Blend all ingredients in the Vita-Mix to a smooth sauce consistency, adding a little water if too thick. Makes 1½ cups.

Guacamole

4 large avocadoes
½–1 cup chopped cilantro
2 minced green onions
2–4 cloves garlic, minced or pressed
1 tsp Mexican Seasoning Mix
(see Seasoning Powders)
¼ cup lemon or lime juice
Bragg's or Celtic sea salt to taste

This recipe is quite versatile. Experiment with your options!

Mash avocados then add all other ingredients. If storing in the fridge, place an avocado seed in the mixture—this will help deter oxidation. You can also squeeze additional lemon juice on top.

Variations: Add diced tomatoes, red bell peppers, or grated zucchini to the basic recipe. If you do this, you may want to adjust the seasonings.

Spicy Fruit Sauce

4 Medjool dates, soaked 2 hours
¼ cup fresh-squeezed orange juice
¼ cup lemon or lime juice
1 Tbs olive oil
1 tsp minced jalapeño pepper

This sauce is wonderful served over any fruit salad.

Blend all ingredients and serve. Makes ¾ cup.

Mango Date Sauce

1 large ripe mango, peeled and cut into chunks
4 Medjool dates, soaked 4 hours
1 Tbs lemon juice
Water to blend

This makes a nice sauce for mixed fruit salads, or try it as a garnish dribbled on the plate around any exotic dessert.

Remove pits from the dates and blend all ingredients in the Vita-Mix until smooth. Makes 1½ cups.

Blackberry/Blueberry Fruit Sauce

2 cups fresh or frozen blackberries or blueberries
¼ cup agave syrup or to taste
¼–½ tsp minced jalapeño (optional)

Berries, especially blueberries, are proving to contain some of the highest antioxidants of all fruits and vegetables. This is also a wonderful food for improving our vision. This fruit sauce is simple and has a little bite to it if you choose to make it with the jalapeño. Try making this with other berries for variety.

Blend all together. Garnish crepes with Coconut Cream (optional, see Yogurt, Creams, and Cheeses).

Macadamia Banana Fruit Sauce

1 banana
¼ cup soaked macadamia nuts
Dash of agave syrup or honey to sweeten
Dash of cinnamon

This recipe makes a nice addition to any fruit salad mixture. Dehydrate the leftovers as patties to make delicious crepes.

Blend all ingredients in the blender and serve over any fruit salad. Makes 1 cup.

Black Mission Fig Sauce

*½ cup Black Mission fig paste
or 1 cup figs, soaked and drained*

1 cup orange juice

This densely mineralized sweet fruit has one of the highest concentrations of calcium of any food. These figs have a laxative and mucus-dissolving effect in the body and are one of the most alkaline fruits available to us. This sauce is delicious served with fruit salads or as a garnish with sorbets or ice creams.

Blend together and serve. Makes 1½ cups.

Calimyrna Fig Sauce

*1 cup Calimyrna figs,
soaked overnight*

⅔ cup fresh-squeezed orange juice

Delicious on fruit salads or as a fruit sauce for garnishing.

Blend all together until smooth. Makes 1½ cups.

Wasabi Sauce

¼ cup Nama Shoyu
¼ cup raw organic sesame oil
1–2 tsp wasabi powder or paste
½ tsp ground flax meal (optional)

This is a classic sauce served with sushi rolls, wraps, or spring rolls. Wasabi is a horseradish root that is quite hot. It can be bought as a green paste in a tube or in powdered form, to which one adds a little water. Either one is great for sushi.

Blend all ingredients until you achieve a smooth consistency. Makes ½ cup.

Ginger Shoyu Sauce

Olive Dulse Tapenade

4–6 cloves of garlic
1 cup black olives
1/4 cup olive oil
1/3 cup dulse flakes

In a food processor, chop garlic and olives then add oil and dulse. You can also do this by hand by mincing the garlic and olives and then mixing in the dulse and oil. This is delicious served with any cracker or bread, or it can be spread on thin slices of jicama and dehydrated (as in the Garlicky Bread recipe—see Side Dishes). Makes 1 cup.

Ginger Shoyu Sauce

1/4 cup raw organic sesame oil
1/4 cup Nama Shoyu
1–2 tsp minced ginger
1 clove garlic
2 Tbs lemon juice
1 Tbs honey or agave syrup

This is a nice accompaniment to the Spring Rolls or Wraps, or it can be used as a marinade or dip with the Shishkabobs.

Blend all ingredients together until the mix attains a smooth consistency and serve. Yields 1/2 cup.

Moroccan Hot Sauce

2 dried Ancho or California chiles, soaked in hot water for 30 minutes
2 Tbs olive oil
3 Tbs lemon juice
1/3 cup water
1 Tbs paprika
1 1/2 tsp jalapeño
1 tsp coriander
1/2 tsp cumin
1/4 tsp black peppercorns, ground fine

This sauce should be made a week before you want to serve it. It makes a nice condiment with the Couscous or as a hot sauce for any dish, if you like it hot. Ancho chiles are 3-4 inches long and triangular in shape.

Boil some water and let sit for a few minutes before soaking chiles. Soak until soft then place chiles and all ingredients into the Vita-Mix and blend well. Store in a glass container in the fridge. This recipe will keep for one month or more. Makes 2/3 cup.

These you can buy already-made from Frontier Foods (see Resources list for ordering information) or make your own.

Tomato Powder

Tomatoes

This can be used instead of soaking sun-dried tomatoes. It makes a great tomato paste or sauce and adds flavor to any Italian dish.

Slice tomatoes very thinly and dehydrate until dry. Grind into a powder in the Vita-Mix, storing in cool dry place.

Jicama Powder

Jicama

Grate jicama, dehydrate, and grind in the Vita-Mix. This makes a wonderful substitute for sugar and does not affect the blood sugar levels like commercial sugars do. Add it to your recipes instead of honey or agave syrup unless you need a chewy texture, in which case jicama would not work.

Tomato Seasoning Mix

¼ cup Tomato Powder
¼ cup Red Bell Pepper Powder
¼ cup onion powder

If you want a quick seasoning to flavor any seed cheese, try this combination.

Mix all ingredients together and store in a cool dry place. Makes ¾ cup.

Seasoning Blend

¹/₄ cup onion powder
¹/₄ cup kelp powder
¹/₄ cup dried basil
1 Tbs garlic powder

Mix all ingredients together and store in glass container in a cool dry place. Makes ³/₄ cup.

Gomasio

1 cup sesame seeds, soaked overnight
1 Tbs garlic cloves, minced
1 Tbs ginger, minced
Celtic sea salt, dulse, or kelp
Cayenne pepper

This makes a tasty topping for salads and is full of calcium.

Dehydrate sesame seeds until dry and crunchy. Grind in the Vita-Mix with sea salt, dulse, or kelp and the garlic and ginger. Taste this and add more ginger and garlic if it is to your taste. If the mixture is too moist then dehydrate for about 2 hours by spreading it out on a teflex sheet. Store in the fridge or freezer. This will usually keep for about one week in the fridge and is a great garnish to sprinkle on salads or soups. Makes 1 cup.

Gremolata

10 garlic cloves, minced
¹/₂ cup firmly packed minced fresh parsley
1 Tbs lemon zest

This tastes great as a garnish with any dish.

Mix together and keep in fridge. Will last two weeks.

Mixed Italian Seasoning

¹/₄ cup dried oregano
¹/₄ cup dried basil
¹/₄ cup dried thyme
¹/₄ cup dried marjoram
¹/₄ cup dried rosemary
1–2 tsp garlic powder
2 Tbs Tomato Powder

This mixture will last for ages if kept in a cool dry place. You can dehydrate any of your own seasonings or get them from Frontier (see Resources list). I think Frontier sells an Italian mix, although I prefer this one.

Mix all ingredients together and store in a cool dry place. Makes 1 cup.

Indian Spice Mix

¼ cup cumin
¼ cup turmeric
¼ cup curry
¼ cup lime zest
¼ cup paprika
1 Tbs cinnamon
1 Tbs nutmeg

Mix all together and store in a covered container in a cool dry place.

Mexican Seasoning Mix

¼ cup oregano
¼ cup cumin
¼ cup chili powder
2 Tbs garlic powder
2 Tbs onion powder

Mix all together and store in a covered container in a cool dry place.

Crispy Garlic Chips

3 bulbs of garlic, separated into cloves and peeled
1 recipe Simple Marinade (see Marinades and Dressings)

This makes a nice garnish for many dishes.

Slice garlic very thin and marinate overnight in the Simple Marinade. Drain and spread out on a teflex sheet and dehydrate until crispy. Use as a garnish or grind up for seasoning.

Tomatillo Bits

Tomatillos

Slice tomatillos very thin and place on dehydrator tray. Dehydrate until dry and crunchy. These make great snacks or as a garnish on soups or salads.

Lemon/Lime and Orange Zest

Lemons or limes
Oranges

Peel the outer skins from the oranges and lemons, using as much as you like. Dehydrate them on the mesh dehydrator trays until dry. You can grind them in a coffee grinder or Vita-Mix (depending on how much you have made) or keep the dehydrated pieces in a cool dry container and grind them when needed. That way they will stay fresh. It would be best to grind these separately so you can have the advantage of either flavor.

Beet Powder

Beets

I like to use this with seed sauces when I want to create a spectacular color contrast for presentation purposes. It is truly amazing.

Grate beets and dehydrate until dry. Grind in a seed grinder or the Vita-Mix if making a larger quantity. Store in a plastic baggie in a cool dry place. This is delicious mixed with the basic seed cheese and will give it an incredible color.

Red Bell Pepper Powder

Red bell peppers

Remove seeds and stem from peppers. Chop peppers in half and place in the Vita-Mix. Pulse-chop into a mushy mixture. You may want to add a tablespoon of water to get the mixture turning. Spread on your teflex sheets and dehydrate until dry and crunchy, then grind into a fine powder using the Vita-Mix. Store in a cool dry place.

Fruit Pie

Desserts

Pies and Cakes

Pie Crusts

Pie crusts for desserts are usually sweet, as the best ones are made from a combination of fruits, nuts, dates, and seasonings. Feel free to be creative and come up with your own combinations.

Note: When making crusts, if they appear too wet, then place them in the dehydrator for 2–3 hours to firm up, or add a couple of teaspoons of psyllium husks.

Pie Fillings

These are simple, consisting of whatever fruits are in season, dates to sweeten, and psyllium to thicken. You can frost your pie with either Macadamia Nut Cream Frosting or Cashew Nut Cream Frosting (See Frostings section, next).

Note: When using dates to sweeten, make sure to pit and soak them in a little water to soften.

Crust:

3 cups almonds, soaked overnight and dehydrated 2 hours

2 cups honey or Medjool dates, soaked 1 hour to soften

1 cup shredded coconut

Filling:

6 cups strawberry puree

2 cups soaked dates to sweeten

6 Tbs psyllium

Process almonds in a food processor until mealy. Add in dates and coconut to form a dough. Press into a springform pan and set aside.

Blend strawberries and dates together until smooth. Add in psyllium to thicken. Pour onto crust and place in the fridge to set. Garnish with cashew or macadamia nut frosting (see Frostings section, next). Slice fresh strawberries on top just before serving.

Variation: Make a crust and press into a springform pan. Make a thick mixed Cashew/Macadamia Nut Cream Frosting, with 1 tsp psyllium husk added to it. Spread this frosting directly over the crust. Slice strawberries in half and coat lightly with honey or agave syrup. Place strawberries in a spiral design on the frosting "filling" and thus over the top of the pie. Chill and serve. Garnish with a little Chocolate Mint Sauce and Coconut Cream Frosting (see Frostings).

Crust:

2 cups Calimyrna figs, soaked overnight and chopped

1 cup almonds, soaked overnight and dehydrated 2 hours

1 cup walnuts

1/2 cup chopped walnuts, set aside

1/2 cup coconut

Filling:

1 cup dates, soaked until soft

2 cups papaya chunks

1 banana

1 mango, peeled and sliced

2 limes, juiced

1/2 tsp lemon zest

1/2 tsp ginger

1/8 tsp minced jalapeño

4 Tbs psyllium husks

This recipe is a delicious blend of fruits and nuts that will leave the taste buds wanting more.

Place almonds and walnuts in food processor and process until mealy in texture. Add figs slowly until all are mixed in with the nuts. Transfer to a large bowl and mix in chopped walnuts and coconut. Pat into a pie plate with your fingers, bringing the crust up the sides and fluting the edges. If you have leftovers, roll these into balls and chill. They make delicious candy treats.

Blend all the filling ingredients together and set aside. Now alternate the following fruits, placing a layer of filling between each layer of fruit.

First layer: sliced bananas; second layer: sliced strawberries; third layer: sliced pears, plums, papaya, etc. Use your imagination when choosing your fruits. I like to end with mango swirls on top and sliced strawberries around the outside of the pie. Chill 2 hours to set.

207

Crust:

1 cup Black Mission figs,
soaked overnight

1 cup organic Turkish apricots,
soaked overnight

1 Red Delicious apple,
peeled and grated

2 cups pecans or walnuts,
coarsely ground

Filling:

2 bananas

4 cups chopped ripe papaya

2 cups chopped pineapple

4 Tbs psyllium

1 cup honey dates (optional)

In a food processor, grind walnuts or pecans until mealy and set aside. Place figs, apricots, and apples in food processor and process until pureed. Add to walnuts and mix well. Pat mixture into the bottom of a springform pan. If mixture is too wet, add 1–2 tsp psyllium.

Blend the three fruits and psyllium together and set aside. If you have a real sweet tooth then add the dates when blending; otherwise it's sweet enough as is. Now layer the pie crust with sliced fruits of your choice, pouring an equal amount of filling between each layer.

Choices of fruit that work well are strawberries, bananas, peaches, mangos, papayas, apples, persimmons, pineapple, raspberries, blueberries, or anything else that may be in season. I like to use at lease three different fruits and then make the top layer decorative. Place in the fridge to set at least 2 hours.

Variation: Blackberry Banana Filling

Combine 3 cups blackberries, 2 bananas, and ½–1 cup soaked dates, along with 4 Tbs psyllium.

Avocado Banana Fruit Pie

Crust:

*2 cups dried Calimyrna figs
or apricots*

1 banana

Filling:

1 avocado

5 bananas

¼ tsp vanilla or vanilla bean*

Agave syrup or honey to taste

*Garnish: peaches, mangos,
strawberries, raspberries, bananas,
or other fresh fruit*

Soak figs or apricots in water until softened. Combine with one fresh banana and blend in the Vita-Mix or food processor. Pat into glass pie plate and dehydrate until firm.

Note: Rub a small quantity of olive oil on pie plate before adding the crust. This will prevent it from sticking.

Blend all filling ingredients together and pour into pie crust. Place in freezer to set firm. Garnish with assorted fresh fruits of your choice. You can be very creative with how you arrange the fruit topping.

***Note:** Many of the dessert recipes use vanilla. Because I live in Mexico, I can purchase some of the very best vanilla extracts, so I usually choose to use them over the actual bean. When making the conversion from vanilla extract to a fresh vanilla bean, use two inches of vanilla bean to 1 teaspoon vanilla extract, then blend or mix in as the recipe indicates.

209

Mango Apricot Pie

Crust:

2 cups pecans

2 cups walnuts

1 cup shredded unsweetened coconut

2 cups Medjool dates, soaked to soften

Filling:

*2 cups dried orange apricots soaked
overnight (you can also use fresh
apricots here when they are in season)*

4 cups mango, peeled and chopped

2 cups honey dates, soaked 1 hour

6 Tbs psyllium

This blend of nuts and fruits will keep your taste buds guessing.

In a food processor grind pecans, walnuts, and coconut together until mealy. Slowly add in dates until a doughy consistency is met. Pat mixture no less than ¼ inch thick into a springform pan.

In a food processor or Vita-Mix, blend the apricots and mango together, slowly adding in the dates. Mix in the psyllium, then pour onto crust. Let set in the fridge for 2 hours before serving. Garnish top with sliced mangos and sliced fresh apricots. Serve with Coconut Cream Frosting (see Frostings section).

Garnish with fresh mango and apricots.

Crust:

2 cups almonds, soaked and dehydrated 2 hours

1 cup Medjool dates, soaked 1 hour to soften

¼ tsp vanilla

¼ tsp cinnamon

Date soaking water if necessary

Filling:

2 cups pumpkin puree

1–1½ cups dates, soaked 1 hour

¼ cup raisins, soaked 1 hour

½ cup cashews, soaked 4 hours

2 persimmons, peeled

2 sapotes

½–1 tsp cinnamon

1–2 tsp vanilla

¼ tsp cloves

¼ tsp nutmeg

¼ tsp cardamom

Raisin or date soaking water

3 Tbs psyllium

Dash of Celtic sea salt

Garnish:

1 recipe Macadamia Nut Cream (see Frostings)

Try this alternative at your next Thanksgiving dinner.

Place almonds in food processor and process until mealy. Slowly add in dates, water, vanilla, and cinnamon to form a dough consistency. Pat into a glass pie plate so that crust is at least ¼ inch thick.

To make pumpkin puree, put peeled and chopped pumpkin through the Champion juicer with the blank in place. Then run the dates, raisins, and nuts through the Champion juicer, again with the blank attachment. Combine the two then add the mixture to the Vita-Mix, along with the remaining ingredients (except for the psyllium husks). Use just enough soaked raisin water to keep the blades turning. Remove mixture to a larger bowl and stir in psyllium husks. This will help to firm the pie so that it slices neatly. Scoop mixture into the crust and chill 2 hours before serving. Garnish with Macadamia Nut Cream Frosting.

Crust:

2 cups pecans

2 cups walnuts

*½ cup shredded
unsweetened coconut*

1 cup raw rolled oat groats

¼ cup olive oil

⅓ cup agave syrup or honey

Filling:

2 cups white figs, soaked overnight

2 bananas

2 apples, peeled, cored and chopped

1 Tbs psyllium

In a food processor grind pecans, walnuts, coconut, and oats together until mealy. Slowly add in oil and agave syrup until a doughy consistency is met. Pat into pie pan no less than ¼ inch thick. Dehydrate if too wet about 2–3 hours.

In a food processor blend all ingredients and fill crust. Dehydrate 6 hours. Garnish top with fresh sliced mangos and fresh sliced figs. Serve with Coconut Cream Frosting (see Frostings).

211

Apple Cranberry Pie and Ice Cream

Crust:

2 cups ground walnuts

2 cup pecans, ground

1 cup raisins, soaked 2 hours

1 cup honey or Medjool dates, soaked 1 hour

Filling:

10–12 peeled and chopped apples

2 cups dates, soaked until soft

1 cup dried cranberries, soaked 2 hours (you can also use fresh)

½ cup soaked raisins

2 tsp cinnamon

¼ tsp nutmeg

2 Tbs lemon juice

4–6 Tbs psyllium

1 recipe Vanilla Almond Ice Cream

Drain soaked fruit and set aside. In a food processor process the walnuts and pecans until mealy, slowly adding in the soaked raisins and dates to form a dough consistency. If dough is too wet, add in 2 tsp psyllium. Pat into a springform pan, making the crust no less than ¼ inch thick.

In a food processor or Vita-Mix blend apples, dates, cranberries, raisins, lemon juice, cinnamon, and nutmeg. When thoroughly mixed, blend in psyllium. Scoop onto pie crust and chill until set. Serve with Vanilla Almond Ice Cream (see Ice Creams, below).

Note: If using fresh cranberries, adjust the sweetener, as cranberries can be quite tart.

212

Banana Coconut Cream Pie

Crust:

2 cups almonds or pecans, soaked overnight and dehydrated 2 hours

¼ cup agave syrup or ½ cup soaked dates

¼ cup coconut, shredded

Filling:

5–6 frozen bananas

1½ cups frozen coconut meat from a young coconut

¼ cup dates, soaked until soft then frozen

1 tsp vanilla

Garnish:

1 cup shredded coconut

½ cup chopped beets, juiced

This delicious creamy pie will melt in your mouth, taking you on a trip to far-away tropical islands. Yummmmm.

In a food processor grind almonds until mealy, slowly adding in the agave syrup or dates. Remove from processor and fold in shredded coconut. Pat into pie plate.

Run all the filling ingredients through the Champion with the blank attachment and fill crust. Freeze. Defrost 15 minutes before serving and garnish. Mix just enough beet juice with coconut to add color, then dehydrate until dry and crunchy. Sprinkle coconut on pie just before serving.

Variation: Chocolate Coconut Cream Pie

Add 1 cup cacao powder (or carob powder) to Banana Coconut Cream Pie and follow recipe as above.

Pineapple Coconut Cream Pie

Crust:

See Banana Coconut Cream Pie, above.

Filling:

4 cups frozen chopped pineapple

2 frozen bananas

1½ cups frozen young coconut meat

½ cup dates

2 tsp pineapple extract

Run all ingredients through the Champion with the blank attachment and fill crust. Freeze. Defrost 15 minutes before serving and garnish with chopped fresh pineapple and grated coconut.

Strawberry Cheesecake

Crust:

2 cups soaked figs

2 cups soaked dates

1 cup walnuts

½ cup agave syrup or honey

2 tsp vanilla extract

2 Tbs cacao powder or carob powder

Filling:

2 cups frozen strawberries

2 cups walnuts

1 cup Coconut Cream Frosting (optional—see Frostings)

½–¾ cups agave syrup or honey

2 Tbs vanilla

Process walnuts in a food processor until mealy. Set aside. Puree rest of ingredients and add to walnuts. Pat into a pie plate or springform pan to make a crust. Dehydrate the crust until firm.

In the Vita-Mix blend strawberries, walnuts, ½ cup Coconut Cream Frosting, agave syrup, and vanilla. Blend until smooth and creamy. Pour into pie crust and place in the freezer. Thaw slightly before serving. Garnish with sliced fresh strawberries, mint leaves, and Coconut Cream Frosting on top.

Pineapple Cheesecake

Crust:

¾ cup Black Mission figs, soaked 2 hours in ½ cup water

½ cup dates, soaked 2 hours

5 dried pineapple rings, soaked ½ hour

1½ Tbs cacao powder or carob powder

1 cup coarsely ground walnuts

½ cup walnut pieces

½ cup raisins, soaked 2 hours to soften

½ cup grated coconut

½ tsp cinnamon

This is a fabulous recipe for "cheesecake," and all the credit for this one goes to the Optimum Health Institute guest who came to me one day with a taste of this. I wish I could remember her name, but if she sees this recipe she will know. I want to thank you so much for sharing this with me. Enjoy!

Drain soaked fruit and reserve water. Use a food processor and process walnuts until coarsely ground. Set aside. Next, process figs, dates, and cacao powder with a little reserved water. Place in a large bowl. Cut pineapple into small pieces and add to pureed fig/date mixture. Add in the walnuts, raisins, coconut, and cinnamon, making a dough. Pat crust into the bottom of a springform pan. Dehydrate if necessary to create a firm crust (no more than 3 hours).

Filling:

2½ cups cashews, soaked 5 hours

1 small papaya

1 soft pear or sapote, seeded

1 cup Medjool dates, soaked 2 hours to soften

1 fresh pineapple, hold juice

2 tsp pineapple extract

2 tsp vanilla

4 Tbs psylliym husks or 4 Tbs agar agar

Put pineapple through the Champion juicer with the blank, catching any juice that is released. Follow with papaya, pear or sapote, and dates. Add all the ingredients to the Vita-Mix and blend, adding in the extracts. If you choose to use psyllium husks to thicken, add this last. Agar agar is another thickening agent that can be used, but it usually needs to be boiled to dissolve the crystals. For this recipe you could heat the remaining pineapple juice with just enough water to dissolve the agar-agar. Then add back to the remaining ingredients.

Spread mixture on top of crust in your springform pan and dehydrate for 6 hours. Let pie cool then remove springform sides to add the topping.

Pineapple Coconut Topping

1 recipe Cashew Nut Cream Frosting (see Frostings)
1 cup fresh pineapple, cut into small chunks
½ cup shredded, unsweetened coconut

With a spatula, spread the Cashew Nut Cream Frosting on the top and sides of the cheesecake. Garnish with pineapple chunks and sprinkled coconut. Serve immediately or chill.

215

Chocolate Cake

2 cups Black Mission figs,
soaked overnight

2 cups Turkish apricots,
soaked overnight

6 apples, peeled, cored and chopped

⅔ cup cacao powder
or carob powder

1 tsp vanilla

Combine all ingredients in a food processor and blend until smooth. Pat into a springform pan and dehydrate until firm, approximately 6–8 hours. Remove sides of pan, and continue to dehydrate another 2 hours. For a double-layered chocolate cake, split the mixture into two equal parts and use two glass pie plates the same size. Put a small bit of olive oil on the pie plates before adding ingredients for easy removal after baking. When one side has dried to a firm texture, flip the cake over carefully to remove pie plate and dehydrate the other side. Layer with Avocado Coconut Chocolate Frosting (see next section), frosting between layers, but not on top. Ice the top of the cake with Macadamia Nut Cream Frosting or Coconut Cream Frosting, and drizzle with Divine Chocolate Sauce just before serving.

Cinnamon Apple Cake with Kiwi Frosting

Cake:

2 cups white figs, soaked overnight

1 cup dried orange apricots,
soaked overnight

3 apples, peeled and grated

2 tsp cinnamon

1–2 Tbs psyllium husks (optional)

Layered Frosting:

2 avocados

2 bananas

4 large kiwi, sliced

In a food processor, puree the figs, apples, and apricots. Add the psyllium husks slowly to help firm the cake dough. Rub a little olive oil on pans for easy removal before transferring the mixture to two glass pie pans, dividing equally. Dehydrate until firm.

Blend avocado and bananas in the Vita-Mix. Spread a layer on top of one of the cakes and cover with sliced kiwi. Gently remove the other cake from the pie pan and place it on top of this layered frosting. Make 1 recipe Macadamia Nut Cream Frosting for the top icing. (Use avocado and fruit frosting for the inner layers.) Garnish with sliced kiwi and a sprinkle of cinnamon.

Cake:

2 cups walnuts

2 cups zucchini, grated

1 cup dates, soaked 2 hours

2 apples, peeled, cored, and chopped

1 tsp cinnamon

¹/₂ tsp nutmeg

¹/₄ cup light olive oil

Topping:

1 box fresh strawberries

*2/3 cup macadamia nuts or cashews,
soaked overnight*

¹/₄ cup agave syrup or honey

1 tsp vanilla

*¹/₄ cup fresh-squeezed orange juice
if needed*

In a food processor grind walnuts until mealy. Set aside. Next process zucchini, dates, apples, spices, and oil, blending well. Scoop into a springform pan or large pie pan and dehydrate 6–8 hours until firm.

Blend strawberries slowly, adding remaining ingredients. If too thick add a little orange juice so that the blades will turn the mixture over. Frost cake and chill for 2 hours. Garnish with fresh sliced strawberries just before serving.

Carrot Cake

Crust:

2 cups ground walnuts

2 cups shredded coconut

*2 cups Medjool dates, soaked
1 hour to soften*

Filling:

6 cups carrot puree

1½ cups carrot juice

2 cups young coconut meat

2 cups Medjool dates, soaked 1 hour

1-inch chunk of ginger

1 cup raisins, soaked 1 hour

1½ tsp cinnamon

1 tsp cardamom

1 tsp nutmeg

6–8 Tbs psyllium

Icing:

*1 recipe Macadamia Nut
Cream Frosting*

½ cup shredded carrot

Make a crust combining nuts, coconut, and dates. Pat into the bottom of a springform pan, making a crust no less than ¼ inch thick.

Run carrots and ginger through the Champion with the blank in place to make puree. Add to Vita-Mix with all the other ingredients except the psyllium and raisins and blend until smooth. Add in the psyllium and raisins, then pour filling onto crust. Put in the fridge to set for at least 2 hours.

Remove sides of pan and frost with Macadamia Nut Cream Frosting or Cashew Nut Cream Frosting. Sprinkle with shredded carrots and a few soaked raisins and serve.

Pecan Tarts

Crust:

1 cup Brazil nuts, soaked overnight

1 cup walnuts, soaked overnight

*2/3 cup Black Mission fig paste
or 1 cup Black Mission figs,
soaked 2 hours*

Filling:

1 cup pecans, soaked 1 hour

2/3 cup water

*6–8 Medjool dates, soaked
1 hour to soften*

1 tsp vanilla

1–2 Tbs psyllium

Topping:

1 cup pecans

2 Tbs honey or agave syrup

Dash of Nama Shoyu or Bragg's

1 Tbs water

Drain the nuts and set in the dehydrator for two hours at 105 degrees. In a food processor, process the nuts until mealy and slowly add in the fig paste or soaked figs one at a time until mixture starts to form into dough. Add a little water if necessary. Remove from the food processor and make small 4-inch rounds approximately 3/4 inch thick on teflex sheets. Make a slight indentation for the filling by pressing with the fingertips all around the mound. This should look like a tart shell. Dehydrate for 4 hours at 105 degrees.

Blend in the Vita-Mix all the ingredients until a fine creamy consistency is formed. Pour into the center of the tarts and dehydrate for another 2 hours or until set.

Mix together honey or agave syrup, shoyu or Bragg's, and water , and mix with pecans until well coated. Arrange on top of the tarts and chill. Serve with Coconut Cream Frosting or Vanilla Almond Ice Cream.

Frostings

Coconut Cream Frosting

3–4 mature coconuts

Honey or agave syrup to sweeten

1 tsp vanilla

1 tsp coconut extract (optional)

This simple recipe makes one of my favorite frostings. If you choose to use this, then chill it first so that it stiffens a little.

Drain the water from the coconuts and split open with a machete. Using a butter knife, remove the hard white coconut meat. Cut into pieces that will fit through your Champion juicer with the screen attachment. Juice the coconut meat. A thick white cream will be extracted that is one of the most amazing-tasting foods just by itself. Add a little honey or agave syrup if you want to sweeten this, along with the rest of the ingredients. Chill. Makes 1 cup.

Peppermint Prune Whip

1 cup pitted prunes, soaked overnight

1 cup nut frosting made from macadamia nuts, cashews, or coconut (see recipes in this section)

¼ tsp vanilla

Agave syrup or honey to taste

¼ tsp peppermint extract or 1 Tbs fresh peppermint leaves, minced

Blend prunes, vanilla, peppermint, and agave syrup together. Gently fold in your nut cream and add a little water if necessary to achieve the desired consistency.

Chocolate Frosting

1 recipe Coconut Cream Frosting or other nut cream frosting

1/3 cup cacao powder or carob powder

1/4 cup Turkish apricots, soaked overnight (save water)

Puree apricots in just enough of the soak water to keep the blades turning. Add apricot puree to Coconut Cream Frosting and mix thoroughly. Sift in the cacao powder (to avoid lumping) and mix well. Chill until ready to use. Makes 1½ cups.

Divine Chocolate Sauce

1/2 cup olive oil

1 Tbs vanilla

1 cup cacao powder or ground cocoa beans or carob powder

2 cups agave syrup or honey

If you don't want to use agave syrup then use 1 cup soaked dates to sweeten. This sauce will keep forever in the fridge.

Note: Rawfood.com sells raw cacao beans, which can be pulverized and used instead of cacao. It's extremely high in antioxidants.

Chocolate Mint Sauce

1 recipe Divine Chocolate Sauce (above)

1/4–1/2 tsp peppermint extract

Combine the two and keep chilled.

Fudge Sauce

1/2 cup raw almond butter

1/4 cup cacao powder or carob powder

1/4 cup agave syrup or honey

1 tsp Nama Shoyu

Water

Blend all together, adding water to achieve desired consistency.

These frostings are easy to make. Simply soak your nuts overnight, drain, and blend with a liquid like fresh fruit juice, sweeten with a little honey or agave syrup, and add an extract if desired.

If you are using coconut, buy young spoon-meat coconuts that have rubbery meat inside them. This can then be blended with soaked dried figs, apricots, mangos, prunes, or just about any dried fruit that has been soaked, and a little vanilla. Usually the fruit will sweeten the coconut meat, or you can add agave syrup or honey.

Macadamia Nut Cream Frosting

1½ cups macadamia nuts, soaked overnight
½ cup fresh orange juice, papaya juice, or coconut water
¼ cup agave syrup or honey
1 tsp almond extract

Blend all ingredients in the Vita-Mix until smooth and creamy.

Variation: Cashew Nut Cream Frosting

Make the same as above but use 1½ cups cashews in place of macadamia nuts, and vanilla extract instead of almond extract.

Avocado Coconut Chocolate Frosting

1 avocado
Young coconut meat from 1 coconut
¼ cup cacao powder or carob powder
Agave syrup or honey to taste

Blend all ingredients together until smooth.

Ice Creams

Basic Ice Cream

2 cups cashews, soaked overnight

3 cups water

1 cup coco water

¾ cups young coconut meat

¼–½ cup agave syrup or honey

3 Tbs coconut oil

1 tsp vanilla

For chocolate flavor add ½ cup cacao powder or carob powder

Blend cashews with water and strain through a seed bag. Keep pulp for another occasion. Blend the milk with agave syrup or honey, coconut meat, oil, and vanilla. If making a chocolate ice cream, add in the cacao at this stage and blend. Add to ice cream maker and follow directions to make ice cream, or place in a shallow pie plate or ice trays and freeze. Remove and thaw for 5 minutes or until you can cut into chunks and feed through the Champion juicer with the blank in place. Serve immediately.

Chocolate Ice Cream

1 recipe Basic Ice Cream with cacao powder

Sweeten to taste with agave syrup or honey

Process in ice cream maker or pour into shallow pan and freeze. Follow directions above for Basic Ice Cream.

Vanilla Almond Ice Cream with Honeyed Nuts

2 cups soaked almonds, blanched

2 cups water

1 cup coconut water

½ cup young coconut meat

¼–½ cup agave syrup or honey

2 Tbs coconut oil

2 tsp vanilla

Blend all ingredients in Vita Mix and process in ice cream maker or freeze in shallow pie plates or ice trays. Remove from freezer and pass through the Champion with the blank in place (after thawing for a few minutes and cutting into appropriate-size chunks). Add in Honeyed Nuts (see Cookies, Bars, and Other Treats).

Honeyed Bananas
with Vanilla Almond Ice Cream

3 bananas sliced lengthwise

3 Tbs honey

1/2–1 tsp cinnamon

3 Tbs light olive oil

3 Tbs orange juice

1 tsp Orange Zest
(see Seasoning Powders)

1 recipe Vanilla Almond Ice Cream

Garnish with slivered almonds

Mix honey, cinnamon, olive oil, orange juice, and Orange Zest together. Brush both sides of sliced bananas with this mixture, coating them well. Place on teflex sheets. Reserve remaining mixture. Dehydrate bananas until dry and sticky, then turn over and dehydrate the underside. Serve with ice cream and garnish with reserved sauce and slivered almonds.

Frozen Fruit Creams

2 cups fresh fruit: banana, peach, strawberry, mango, etc.

1 cup cashews, soaked overnight

Coconut water for consistency

This dessert is a little heavier than a sorbet but has the consistency of an ice cream.

Blend nuts and fruits together, adding a little coconut water if necessary to keep the blades turning. Add to ice cream machine, or pour into shallow pie pan or ice trays and freeze. Remove from freezer and cut into chunks. Run through the Champion juicer with the blank in place. This is like a soft-serve ice cream. Enjoy immediately.

Sorbets

These are like ice creams but lighter. They are primarily made from fruits and can be flavored or sweetened to taste. Try using any fruit that is in season; blend with a little banana to give it that sweet and creamy consistency. Note that sorbet is creamy and usually made with bananas; sherbet is more of an ice milk.

Mango Sorbet

3 mangoes, chopped and frozen
1 banana, frozen
Honey to taste (optional)

Run frozen fruits through the Champion with the blank in place, sweeten if necessary, and serve immediately. Serves 2.

Variation: Peach Sorbet, Strawberry Sorbet, Blackberry Sorbet, etc. Use 3 cups frozen fruit to 1 or more bananas. Run through the Champion juicer with the blank and serve immediately.

Strawberry Sorbet

1 box frozen strawberries
1 frozen banana
Honey or agave syrup to taste

Run strawberries and banana through the Champion with the blank, and sweeten as necessary.

Variation: Fruit Sherbet

Use any frozen fruit except bananas, and sweeten with honey or agave syrup. Process as above.

Banana Sorbet

4 bananas, frozen

Run bananas through the Champion with the blank.

Ginger Banana Sorbet

4–6 frozen bananas
1-inch chunk of peeled ginger

Run frozen bananas through the Champion juicer with the blank in place. Run the ginger through the juicer, followed by some of the banana puree to get the last bits of ginger that may still be in the housing. Stir the ice cream together and serve with an Apple Walnut Wafer (see Cookies, Bars, and Other Treats).

Pumpkin Parfait

This triple-layered dessert is a must-try! Pumpkin puree is what gives it color and a dominant flavor, but the twin effects of Macadamia Nut Cream Frosting and Pecan Crumble send this dessert over the top.

Pumpkin Puree:

1½ cups pumpkin puree
¼ cup agave syrup or to taste
½ tsp cinnamon and nutmeg combined
1 recipe Macadamia Nut Cream Frosting
1 Tbs psyllium
1 recipe Ginger Banana Sorbet (immediately above)
1 recipe Pecan Crumble (See Cookies, Bars, and Other Treats)

Peel and chop pumpkin and run through the Champion juicer with the blank attachment in place. Add agave syrup, cinnamon, nutmeg, psyllium, and only ¼ cup Macadamia Nut Cream Frosting to pureed pumpkin.

  To assemble, add a scoop of Ginger Banana Sorbet to parfait glasses. Follow with a scoop of Pumpkin Puree, then a scoop of Macadamia Nut Cream Frosting and a little Pecan Crumble. Repeat this procedure, ending with the crumble. Chill in freezer for 30 minutes, then serve immediately.

Napoleon's Parfait

This is a combination of chocolate ice cream, banana sorbet, and strawberry sorbet with ground-up pecans between the layers (the Pecan Crumble recipe in the Cookies, Bars, and Other Treats section). It is so good! To build the parfait, alternate the three different layers of chocolate, banana, and strawberry ice creams described above, using the Pecan Crumble between each layer and sprinkled on top. Garnish with a fresh strawberry. Serves 4.

Eskimo Pie

Cookie Crust:
1 cup dates, soaked 4 hours
1 cup figs, soaked 4 hours
2 Tbs cacao powder or carob powder
2 Tbs agave syrup or honey
¼ cup dried shredded coconut
1 tsp vanilla

Filling:
1 recipe Mango Sorbet

This is the raw version of the Eskimo Pie ice cream treats sold in supermarkets and eaten by kids everywhere.

Blend all these in a Vita-Mix to make a doughy consistency. Make small circles about 3 inches in diameter on a teflex sheet and dehydrate until chewy. Flip over and dehydrate the underside.

Make Mango Sorbet according to recipe above and set aside in freezer until firm but not stiff. Place a scoop of sorbet about ½ inch thick on cookie crust. Place another cookie on top. Wrap in plastic wrap and freeze until ready to serve. Let thaw for five minutes before serving time. Delicious!

Puddings

This simple dessert can be made by blending the soft spoon meat from the young coconut with any kind of fruit or soaked dried fruit.

Mango Pudding

1 cup soft spoon meat
1 cup mango

Blend together and serve. Makes 2 cups. Try this using other kinds of fresh or dried fruits that have been soaked.

Rainbow Pudding

1 banana
1 cup blueberries
1 mango
1 persimmon
1 cup strawberries
Dash of nutmeg

Run the fruits through the Champion juicer with the blank in place. Catch the fruit in a large bowl. Swirl and lightly blend in the colors. Serve in chilled parfait glasses or small pudding bowls. Sprinkle a little nutmeg on each and garnish with blueberries or other fruit pieces. Serves 2.

Flan

2 cups Coconut Cream Frosting
(see Frostings)
2 Tbs agar dissolved in ½ cup heated
water
½ tsp vanilla
Agave syrup or honey to taste

Dissolve agar agar in boiling water and let sit for 30 minutes. Combine Coconut Cream Frosting, vanilla, and agave syrup. Fold in the agar agar mixture, pour into glass custard cups, and chill. Drizzle agave syrup on top for garnish. Serves 2.

Coconut Custard

1½ cups spoon meat (young coconut
meat)
1 cup Coconut Cream Frosting (see
Frostings)
½ tsp vanilla
2 Tbs agave syrup or honey
Dash of cinnamon
Blend all ingredients in the Vita-Mix.

Garnish with chopped almonds and Orange Zest (see Seasoning Powders). Serves 2.

Fruit & Cream

2 cups chopped papaya
1 cup Coconut Cream Frosting
or Macadamia Nut Cream Frosting
(See Frostings)
Calimyrna Fig Sauce
(see Sauces and Dips)

Similar to a pudding, this dessert offers more texture with chopped fruit.

Gently fold the Coconut Cream Frosting or Macadamia Nut Cream Frosting into the chopped fruit. You can experiment with other kinds of fruit of your choice. Garnish with Calimyrna Fig Sauce.

Cookies, Bars, and Other Treats

Raw cookies are the easiest things to make. You can be very creative in this endeavor by using different combinations of fruits, dried fruits, nuts and/or seeds. Flavoring can be chosen from cinnamon, nutmeg, cardamom, and the extracts. Most commercial extracts do have a little alcohol in them, so try to use the vanilla bean or essential oils that are edible.

Honeyed Nuts

1 cup pecans or walnuts, soaked overnight

1/3 cup agave syrup or honey

Dash of sea salt, cinnamon, and nutmeg

Coat pecans well, spread on a teflex sheet, and dehydrate until sticky-dry. Add into ice cream after processing through the Champion.

Walnut-Raisin-Coconut-Date Cookies

2 cups walnuts, soaked 3 hours

2 cups pecans, soaked 3 hours

1 cup raisins, soaked 1 hour

1–1/2 cup dates, soaked 2 hours

2 tsp vanilla

1 cup grated coconut

After soaking the nuts, put them in the dehydrator for 2 hours. They will grind more easily this way. In a food processor grind the nuts until mealy. Slowly add in the raisins, dates, and vanilla to make a doughy consistency. Use a little of the soaked water if dough is too dry. Remove mixture to a larger bowl and make sure that it is well mixed. Add in the coconut or form into cookie shapes and dip into coconut. Dehydrate until chewy. Flip over to dehydrate the underside. Makes 16 cookies.

Nutty Banana Fruit Cookie

1 cup walnuts, soaked 2 hours
1 cup pecans, soaked 1 hour
5–10 dates, soaked 2 hours
1/2 cup raisins, soaked 1/2 hour
1 large banana
1/4–1/2 cup orange juice
Sprinkle of cinnamon to taste

In a food processor grind nuts, dates, raisins, banana, orange juice, and cinnamon together. Form into cookie-size pieces, no more than 1 inch thick, and place on teflex sheets. Dehydrate for 6–8 hours then flip over to dehydrate the underside for another 6 hours.

Variation: Tropical Mixed Fruit Cookie

Use macadamia nuts or Brazil nuts instead of walnuts, and substitute a mango for the banana; or use both kinds of fruit, adding in a little coconut to make a Tropical Mixed Fruit Cookie.

Oatmeal Raisin Cookies

1 1/2 cups kamut, sprouted
2 cups oat grouts, sprouted
1/2–3/4 cup honey or agave syrup
1 cup dates, soaked 1/2 hour
1 tsp lemon extract
1 tsp vanilla
1/4 cup currants, soaked 1 hour
1/4 cup sunflower seeds, soaked overnight
1/4 cup chopped pecans, soaked 2 hours

To sprout, see Sprouting section earlier in the book.

In a food processor combine the kamut and oats, slowly adding the honey, dates, and extracts. Remove mixture and put in a large bowl. Mix in the currants, sunflower seeds, and pecans. Shape the batter into cookies and place on teflex trays. Dehydrate until crispy or to taste.

Oatmeal Raisin Cookies #2

2 cups ground (raw) rolled oat groats to make a flour

¾ cup raisins, soaked ½ hour (reserve soak water)

1 cup each of walnuts, cashews, and pecans

3 apples, peeled, cored and grated

1 cup grated coconut

¾ cup agave syrup or honey

To make oat groat flour, blend in the Vita-Mix.

In a food processor grind nuts until mealy. Add in the oat flour, apples, soaked raisins, agave syrup, and coconut to make a stiff dough. If too dry, add a little of the soak water. Drop by spoonfuls on a teflex sheet and dehydrate until dry and chewy. Flip over to dehydrate the underside.

Chocolate Brownies

2 cups almond meal (leftover pulp from almond milk)

1 cup dates, soaked 2 hours to soften

1 banana

1 cup pine nuts, soaked overnight

⅓ cup cacao powder or carob powder

1 cup chopped walnuts

1 tsp vanilla

2 Tbs agave syrup or honey

Fudge Sauce (See Frostings)

In a food processor combine nuts, dates, banana, cacao, vanilla, and agave syrup. Add almond meal and process all ingredients until mixed thoroughly. Fold in chopped walnuts and place on teflex sheet, forming batter into a large square no more than 1½ thick. Score into bite-size pieces with a knife and dehydrate 4–6 hours on one side; flip over and dehydrate 4–6 hours on the underside. Frost with Fudge Sauce and serve.

Chocolate Pineapple Squares

*1 cup Black Mission figs,
soaked 2 hours*

½ cup dates, soaked 2 hours

*6 dried pineapple rings,
soaked 1 hour*

1 cup coarsely ground walnuts

½ cup walnut pieces

½ cup raisins, soaked 1 hour

½ cup grated coconut

½ tsp cinnamon

*1½ Tbs cacao powder
or carob powder*

Topping:

2 cups fresh pineapple pulp

3 Tbs agave syrup or honey

This recipe is similar to the crust recipe for the Pineapple Cheesecake. You can also make this recipe into Bliss Balls by rolling the dough in a little shredded coconut or ground-up nuts. When making this recipe, soak the dried fruits in just enough water to cover them.

Drain the soaked fruit and reserve the water. Puree the figs, dates, and cacao powder in a little of the reserved water. Use the Vita-Mix or food processor for this. Add to a larger bowl. In a small food processor or coffee grinder, grind 1 cup walnuts. Add this to the mixture along with the larger walnut pieces. Cut the soaked pineapple into small pieces and add this and the raisins to the mixture. Add in coconut and cinnamon.

Put fresh pineapple through the Champion or Vita-Mix to make 2 cups pineapple pulp, adding the agave syrup if you want it sweeter. Pat cookie dough on a teflex sheet in your dehydrator to make a large square. Spread a layer of pineapple puree over the top of the dough and dehydrate until dry but still chewy. Once the top is somewhat dried you can flip it over by placing another tray on the top and turning it over carefully. Remove tray and dehydrate the underneath side for about 1 hour.

Dream Bars

4 cups ground walnuts

6 cups raw rolled oat groats

1½ cups grated coconut

⅓ cup olive oil

¼ cup agave syrup or honey

2 tsp vanilla

1 recipe Fudge Sauce (See Frostings)

½ cup grated coconut

1 cup pecan halves

In a food processor grind walnuts and raw oats until mealy. Add in coconut, oil, vanilla, and agave syrup. On a teflex sheet pat batter into a large square about ½ inch thick. Dehydrate until chewy. Flip over and dehydrate the bottom side.

Spread chocolate Fudge Sauce on top about ¼ inch thick. Sprinkle with shredded coconut and decorate with pecan halves. Make sure that each square you cut has a pecan half on it. Keep in the freezer.

Blueberry Dream Bars

Crust:

2 cups ground walnuts, pecans, or Brazil nuts or combination

1 cup shredded coconut

2 cups pitted honey dates, soaked 2 hours in 1½ cups water

Filling:

4 cups blueberry puree

1 cup soaked dates or agave syrup to sweeten

3 Tbs psyllium to thicken

Topping:

1 recipe Pecan Crumble (see this section, below)

These are like the traditional date bars but made with blueberries. Researchers are now finding out that blueberries are the tops in antioxidants of all fruits and are an excellent food for improving eyesight.

In a food processor, grind the nuts until mealy, slowly adding in the coconut and dates. This mixture should start to form a dough-like consistency; if not, add a tablespoon or so of water. Press into a springform pan to make a crust about ½ inch thick.

Blend blueberries to make 4 cups puree and add in agave syrup or dates to sweeten. Add psyllium to thicken. Spread this layer about ½ inch thick over the top of the crust layer.

Make Pecan Crumble and sprinkle on top of blueberry layer. Chill for 2 hours, remove sides of springform pan, and cut into triangles. Serve with Basic Ice Cream or a nut cream.

Sesame Flax Bar

1 cup sesame seeds, soaked 2 hours
1 cup flax seeds, soaked 2 hours
in ½ cup water
½ cup sunflower seeds,
soaked overnight
8 dates, soaked 2 hours or until soft
Honey to taste
¼ tsp vanilla
Orange juice or apple juice
to moisten

Mix seeds in a bowl together. Make a paste from the soaked dates with a little vanilla, honey, and orange juice to moisten. Add to the seed mixture and spread into rectangular bars on the teflex sheets in the dehydrator, no higher than ½ inch. Dehydrate for 10 hours on one side at 105 degrees, then dehydrate on the underside for another 8–10 hours. Remove the tray so that the bars are sitting directly on the dehydrator tray now (without the teflex).

Apple Walnut Wafers

2 cup flax seeds, soaked in 4 cups
water for 4 hours
2 cups walnuts
2 apples, peeled, cored and chopped
½ cup dried cherries,
soaked ½ hour
⅓ cup large plump raisins,
soaked ½ hour
¼ cup agave syrup or honey
1 tsp cinnamon
1 tsp vanilla

This is a sweet wafer that is delicious served with any of the sorbets or ice creams.

In a food processor grind walnuts until mealy. Remove and set aside. Next process apples, soaked cherries, raisins, agave syrup, vanilla, and cinnamon. Add in ⅔ of the total amount of flax seeds and process well. Add to walnuts and remaining flax seeds but do not process again. Stir well and spread the mixture ¼ inch thick on a teflex sheet. Dehydrate 8 hours then flip over and dry the underside. Break into cracker-size pieces and serve with ice creams or sorbets. Store in the freezer.

Raw White Chocolate
(from *The Cosmic Pepper Man*)

3/4 cups melted cacao butter

1 1/2 cups coconut butter

3 Tbs tocotrienols

5 Tbs agave syrup or honey

4 Tbs hemp seeds

1 vanilla bean

Thanks to David Steinberg from Rawfood.com, we have the best raw-food chocolate ever, and you can easily purchase all the ingredients right there. See Resources list in the back of the book.

Melt cacao butter in a double boiler at a low temperature. Add in coconut butter and continue to melt, making sure not to heat above 105 degrees. Remove from heat and add to Vita-Mix, along with agave syrup, hemp seeds, and the inner seeds and scrapings from a vanilla bean. Blend thoroughly and pour into shallow molds or a shallow pan. Place in the freezer to set. To remove, let molds sit at room temperature for five minutes.

Variation: Dark Chocolate

Simply add 4 Tbs of raw cacao powder or carob powder to the above recipe and follow the directions.

Fudge Chews

1 recipe Fudge, see below

2 cups macadamia nuts, soaked overnight and dehydrated 2 hours

1 cup shredded dried coconut

2/3 cup raisins, soaked 2 hours

6 Medjool dates, soaked 2 hours

1 tsp vanilla

Chopped pecans

Drain dates and raisins and set aside. Reserve soak water. In a food processor, grind nuts and coconut until mealy. Slowly add in dates, raisins, and vanilla. Add in a little soak water if necessary for moisture. Press mixture 1/2 inch thick into a rectangular glass pan. If you find this too wet then dehydrate before putting Fudge topping on.

237

Fudge

2 cups walnuts, soaked 2 hours
1 cup dates, soaked 2 hours
1/2 cup Coconut Cream Frosting
(See Frostings)
1/2 cup cacao powder
or carob powder
1/4 cup agave syrup or honey
1 tsp vanilla

Run walnuts and dates through the Champion with the blank in place. Fold in Coconut Cream Frosting, cacao powder, agave syrup, and vanilla. Spread fudge 1½ inches thick over crust, and garnish with chopped pecans. Score the fudge into squares and place in the freezer to set, at least 2 hours. Garnish with grated coconut and serve.

Pecan Crumble

2 cups pecans
1/4–1/3 cup agave syrup or honey

Great topping for ice cream and parfaits.

In a food processor, process the pecans until crumbly. Slowly add in the agave syrup to slightly moisten. If it clumps together then dehydrate for a couple of hours until it can crumble between your fingers.

Sesame Flax Bar

Fruit Concoctions

The soft dehydrated fruit rolls below (also called Fruit Leather) are easy to make, and children love them. They are the best substitute for candy but do be aware that any time you dehydrate fruits, the sugar content is more concentrated.

Fruit leathers are made from blended fruits and then spread on a teflex sheet and dehydrated for approximately 48 hours. Store them in a glass container or roll them up and store in a resealable plastic baggie.

Following are some combinations, but be creative and try your own. Do not over-dehydrate or the fruit leather will dry and crack.

Apricot and Nectarine

1 cup apricots, chopped
1 cup nectarines, chopped

Puree both kinds of fruit in the Vita-Mix or blender and spread onto a teflex sheet about ⅛–¼ inch thick. Dehydrate 2 days.

Strawberry Apple

¾ cup strawberries
¾ cup peeled and cored apples
1 Tbs lemon juice

Puree fruits in the blender and spread onto a teflex sheet ⅛–¼ inch thick. Dehydrate for 2 days.

Pineapple Mango

1 cup pineapple, chopped
1 cup mango, chopped

Peel pineapple, making sure to remove all the eyes. Puree both fruits together in the blender and spread onto a teflex sheet ⅛–¼ inch thick. Dehydrate for 2 days.

Fruit Chews

4 bananas
2 large ripe mangoes
4 apples, peeled and grated

Mash bananas and mangoes together. Add grated apples. Drop by spoonfuls on a teflex sheet and dehydrate until chewy. Flip over and dehydrate the underside.

Fruit Chips

bananas, apples, pears, mangos, strawberries, or any other fruit that is in season.

These make great snacks and kids love them. Better still, get the kids to help make them.

Slice fruit no more than ¼ inch thick and dehydrate until dry.

Cinnamon Banana Chips

2 bananas sliced on the diagonal
¼ tsp nutmeg
½ tsp cinnamon

Sprinkle banana slices with cinnamon and nutmeg. Dehydrate on teflex sheet for 16 hours, then turn over and dehydrate the underside.

Raspberry Jam

3½ cups raspberries
2 Tbs lemon juice

Jams and preserves are easy to make and replace the commercial-type jams that are full of sugar and preservatives. To make a jam, simply puree your fruit with a little lemon juice and spread it onto a teflex sheet and dehydrate. The secret here is to stir the fruit every four hours until it reaches the desired thickness. Store in a glass container and refrigerate. Stays fresh for about 2 weeks.

Puree and spread onto teflex sheets. Dehydrate, stirring mixture every four hours until desired thickness. Store in refrigerator.

Variations: Try using strawberries, mango, peaches, or blueberries in this recipe.

Note: If sweetener is needed, add a little date paste or honey.

Papaya Jam

½ Mexican papaya
4 Medjool dates, soaked for 1 hour

With all those wonderful digestive enzymes that papaya has, this jam is especially helpful for anyone with digestive issues. A different version of raw jam, this one is not dehydrated.

Blend papaya and dates together and chill. If you don't have any dates, try a little honey or agave syrup.

Pancakes/Crepes

1 cup macadamia nuts, soaked overnight

3 bananas

Dash of cinnamon

Water

These can be made with just about any nut. The higher-fat-content nuts work better. You can also try other fruits combined with the nuts and come up with your own recipes. Macadamia nuts are very high in selenium, a powerful antioxidant, and the beautifying mineral zinc. Enjoy!

Drain macadamia nuts and place in the Vita-Mix with just enough water to make a smooth thick batter. Blend in bananas and cinnamon. Pour onto teflex sheets in thin round circles about 4 inches in diameter and not more than ¼ inch thick. Dehydrate on one side approximately 2–3 hours, then flip over and dehydrate for another hour, making sure to not over-dry.

To assemble: Spread a layer of Macadamia Nut Cream Frosting or Papaya Jam (see below for the latter; Frostings section for Macadamia Nut Cream Frosting) on top of the crepe, followed by chopped or sliced fruits of your choice. For example, you could use mangoes, strawberries and/or blueberries. Top with Blackberry Fruit Sauce (see Sauces and Dips). Roll the crepe, placing the seam downwards, and drizzle with Coconut Cream (see Yogurt, Creams, and Cheeses) on top. Garnish with chopped walnuts.

Part 4

Final Tidbits

Glossary

Agar-Agar

This is a thickening agent derived from a marine plant. It is best used by dissolving first in boiling water.

Agave Syrup

This is a sweet syrup made from the agave plant (that tequila also is made from). Upon maturity the flowering stalk is cut at the base, where this honey-like syrup is found. It can be used to replace maple syrup or honey as a sweetener in any recipe.

Almonds

These oval-shaped nuts make wonderful milks. They have an alkaline response in the body and provide a good source of calcium. To make them more digestible, soak almonds for one or two days before using. This also helps to remove the tannic acid in the skins.

Apple Cider Vinegar

It must be RAW. This unpasteurized apple cider vinegar has many uses. In this book it is used in the vinaigrette recipes and in some of the marinades. Apple cider vinegar is antiseptic, anti-inflammatory, and improves the secretion of digestive juices. It can be purchased from a health food store.

Arame

This is a seaweed that looks like long black strings. It comes packaged and can be found in the Asian section of health food stores. It needs to be soaked in water before using and provides many nutrients and trace minerals.

Arugula

This dark leafy green has a strong peppery flavor. It can spice up any salad or be used as a garnish. It is a sulfur residue food that when eaten with nuts or avocado digests very well. Sulfur foods are important in the formation of bile acids, which facilitate fat digestion and absorption. It is a beautifying mineral that helps to strengthen connective tissue in the body, thus is essential for hair, nails, and skin. As a dark leafy green it is abundant in chlorophyll, vitamin K, and vitamin B and has an oxygenating effect on the body.

Bananas

Now highly hybridized, bananas no longer have seeds in them and are quite high in sugar content. They are a very good source of potassium so try to find organic; or better still, if you can find the small finger bananas they are naturally sweeter and are the wild variety. Dehydrated they make wonderful snacks for kids.

Black Mission Figs

When fresh, these are small dark figs with a purplish-black skin and reddish interior that has many tiny little seeds. When dried, they lose about two-thirds of their size and become more concentrated in sugar. Fig paste is simply dried Black Mission figs that have been mashed to form a paste. They are a densely mineralized sweet fruit that contains the highest concentration of calcium of any food. Figs are a great laxative and help to dissolve waste and mucus from the intestines.

Bragg's Liquid Aminos

This is a non-fermented liquid amino product made from soybeans. It has a salty flavor and is used in many of the recipes as a salt substitute. It has naturally occurring sodium, but not as much as Nama Shoyu or the average soya sauce.

Buckwheat

This is popularly considered to be a grain, although botanically it is not. It is used as a grain in this recipe book and is high in calcium and protein. When buying buckwheat make sure that you are getting the raw buckwheat groats and not the roasted groats. The grain is light tan in color and triangular in shape.

Cacao Nibs or Powder

A product of the cacao pod, the fruit of the cacao tree, this super-food is what chocolate is made from. The trees grow in warm tropical climates, and the fruit is an elongated pod with the seeds inside, covered with a white fleshy substance. The seeds are dried and broken into pieces (hence nibs) or ground into a powder. Cacao is one of nature's richest sources of magnesium, the brain mineral. It is also a great source of neurotransmitters, which help alleviate depression and give us a sense of well-being.

Cashew Butter

This nut butter is made from raw cashews. Mixed with a liquid it makes a quick creamy base for dressings or soups. You can purchase this at most health food stores.

Cashew Nuts

These are not true raw nuts, due to the process of extracting the seed from the shell. High heat is used, often damaging the life force of the cashew nut itself. Rawfood.com (see Resources list) has the highest-quality raw cashew nut.

Celtic Sea Salt

This is the best sea salt that I know of. Grayish in color, it is high in trace minerals.

Chiles

There are a number of different kinds of chiles, ranging from sweet to heat (with a range of fire power) and widely varying in color, size, and shape—short and narrow, long and skinny, or triangular.

Coconut Butter

This is unrefined coconut oil that has been cooled below 85 degrees. It is a raw saturated fat with many health benefits—see Recommended Reading list (following this Glossary) for *The Miracles of Coconut Oil*. To purchase the best coconut oil (butter), see Rawfood.com, in the Resources and Suppliers section.

Coconut Water

This is the water found inside a fresh coconut. It is full of nutrients and is the purest water that nature provides. The young coconut water is the best for drinking and using as a liquid base in various dishes. Living in Mexico, I buy the fresh young coconuts and open them myself with a machete. This is the best water ever, so full of electrolytes and minerals. If you are in a major U.S. city, you can purchase coconuts at most Asian stores.

Date Paste

This is a paste made from seeded and mashed dates, ideal for sweetening desserts.

Dulse

This purplish seaweed comes in sheets, flakes, or granules. It is a good source of iron and minerals and adds a salty flavor to recipes.

Durian

This amazing fruit grows to be very large, sometimes over 10 pounds. It has a spiky exterior and gives off a sulfurous odor when ripe. It has a light creamy fleshy interior with a few large seeds. It's mostly grown in Malaysia and Indonesia, and if you are lucky, you can sometimes find durian in Asian supermarkets in the U.S. Durian contains high levels of tryptophan, which helps with depression, insomnia, and hypertension. It helps to raise serotonin levels in the brain, and is a strong blood cleanser. It has one of the highest protein contents of any fruit, and is one of the most beautifying foods. Some people find the smell a bit offensive due to the high sulfur content.

Flax Seed

This is a small brown or golden seed, oval in shape and full of the omega-3 and omega-6 essential fatty acid oils. When ground up, it is called flax seed meal and can be added to recipes to thicken and give a nutty flavor.

Galanga

This is a root spice similar to ginger. Found in Asian markets, it is best when purchased fresh. It makes a nice flavor complement to Thai or other Asian dishes.

Ginger

This root vegetable is used extensively in the recipes in this book. I find that small quantities of ginger along with a little garlic and cayenne can really bring out the flavors of the other foods. These spices add a heating element to any dish or juiced drink, which can be helpful if you are trying to live more raw in colder climates.

Goji Berries

Also called wolfberries, these are one of the most nutritionally rich fruits on the planet. They are rosy in color and usually sold dried. They can be soaked and added to smoothies, dressings, or salads or eaten as snacks. Goji berries contain 18 different amino acids, 21 trace minerals, and are one of the richest sources of antioxidant carotenoids (such as beta-carotene). They are also very rich in vitamin C.

Hemp Seed

This very small seed from the hemp plant looks like a tiny nut. It is a complete protein and contains the family of vitamin E, both tocotrenols and tocotrienols. These seeds are very high in antioxidants and essential amino acids, and they also contain lecithin, which is essential for building internal organs. They are wonderful additions to smoothies and salads, or blended into salad dressings. Unfortunately, you can't get them raw in the U.S., since hemp seeds are irradiated when imported.

Jalapeño

This is a small hot chile pepper that is abundant in Mexico. When working with chiles, wear rubber gloves, as the juices can burn the skin. Used with ginger and garlic, this spice can accentuate the flavor of any dish.

Jicama

This is a round root vegetable with a brown skin and a crunchy watery interior. It is very popular in Mexican cuisine and makes a nice addition to any vegetable platter.

Kelp

This is a seaweed that comes powdered or granulated and can be purchased at health food stores. It is high in iodine and many trace minerals and has a bit of a fishy flavor.

Maca

Sometimes called the "Peruvian ginseng," this root vegetable is known to normalize body functions in times of stress, to balance and regulate the hormonal and endocrine systems, and to stimulate fertility, increase energy, and enhance libido. In its dry form maca is ideal to add to cakes, cookies, juices, jams, soups, and other foods. To order, see Rawfood.com in the Resources list.

Medjool Date

These are large meaty dates that are usually quite moist.

Miso

This is a paste made from fermented soybeans; it also can be made with rice or barley. It is usually prepared as a soup. Miso is a good source of protein, B vitamins, enzymes, lactobacillus, calcium, and iron. The varieties include barley, rice, red, golden, black, and white miso.

Nama Shoyu

This is an unpasteurized soy sauce, full of enzymes, and generally less salty than the traditional soy sauce. It comes under the Ohsawa brand and can be purchased at most health food stores.

Nori

This seaweed comes in flat sheets and is used for sushi making in this recipe book. Nori comes both raw and roasted, so try to find the raw kind. Gold Mine sells this product and so does Rawfood.com (see Resources list).

Nutritional Yeast

This yeast product is full of B-complex vitamins and protein. It is found in most health food stores. It's yellowish in color and comes in flakes that are easily sprinkled on various dishes.

Pepita

This is what they call shelled pumpkin seeds in Mexico. The tasty pepita has the highest zinc content of any seed.

Quinoa

This grain from South America, high in the Andes, looks like small grains of millet and is one of the highest-protein grains available.

Tahini

This Middle Eastern nut butter is made from ground sesame seeds. Make sure to buy the raw not roasted kind at the health food store. It provides the body with a good source of calcium and essential fatty acids.

Teflex Sheets

These are the drying sheets used in dehydrators. They have a non-stick surface that makes them perfect for drying crackers, fruit leathers, or any really moist recipe. After items have dried sufficiently on one side, the teflex sheet can be peeled off, the food flipped over, and then the underside dried. The drying sheets are washable and reusable.

Tocotrienol Powder

Also called rice bran powder, this super-food is the bran from the rice seed and the most potent form of vitamin E available. One to two tablespoons per day is recommended as an addition to smoothies, along with all your other super-foods. It is extremely sensitive to heat and easily destroyed. It is very beneficial to the skin and heart.

Tomatillos

These are small green tomatoes with a papery husk covering them. They have a lemony flavor and are a favorite in Mexican cuisine. They grow easily in many parts of North America but are not often sold in stores. You can find them in Mexican markets in southern California.

Turmeric

This root vegetable looks a bit like ginger, and when cut in half it's a bright orange-yellow color. It is popular in Indian and Thai curry dishes, giving any dish that appealing yellow color. Turmeric is widely used in Ayurvedic medicine for its beautifying properties. It has strong anti-inflammatory, anti-oxidant, anti-cancer, and anti-microbial properties. It is also a powerful blood purifier and helps in all skin problems. It is most commonly found in its powdered form, although I like to use the fresh root.

Wasabi Powder

Made from a Japanese horseradish, this condiment has a hot mustard flavor and is served with sushi and raw fish at Japanese restaurants.

Wheatgrass

Grass grown from the wheat berry is a rich source of chlorophyll, vitamins, minerals, amino acids, enzymes, oxygen, and much more. It is known to be one of the most powerful detoxifiers of the body and an evolutionary food.

Recommended
Reading

Arlin, Stephen, Dini Fouad, and David Wolfe. *Nature's First Law: The Raw-Food Diet*. San Diego, CA: Maul Brothers Publishing, 1996.

Arlin, Stephen. *Raw Power! Building Strength & Muscle Naturally*. San Diego, CA: Maul Brothers Publishing, 2000.

Batmanghelidj, Dr. F. *Your Body's Many Cries for Water*. Falls Church, VA: Global Health Solutions, Inc., 1997.

Bragg, Paul. *The Miracle of Fasting*. Santa Barbara, CA: Health Science, 1966.

Calbom, Cherie, and Maureen Keane. *Juicing for Life*. Garden City Park, NY: Avery Publishing Group, 1992.

Clark, Hulda. *The Cure for All Diseases*. San Diego, CA: ProMotion Publishing, 1995.

Cousens, Dr. Gabriel. *Conscious Eating*. Berkeley, CA: North Atlantic Books, 2000.

Emoto, Marasu. *The Hidden Messages in Water*. Translated by David A. Thayne. New York: Atria Books, 2005.

Fife, Bruce. *The Healing Miracles of Coconut Oil*. Colorado Springs, CO: Health Wise Publications 2000.

Garrison, Robert, and Elizabeth Somer. *The Nutrition Desk Reference*. New Canaan, CT: Keats Publishing, 1995.

Gray, Robert. *The Colon Health Handbook*. Emerald Publishing, 1990.

Kulvinskas, Viktoras. *Survival in the 21st Century*. Fairfield, IA: 21st Century Publications, 1975.

Hawkins, David R. *Power vs. Force*. Carlsbad, CA: Hay House, Inc., 1998.

Hay, Louise. *You Can Heal Your Life*. Santa Monica, CA: Hay House, 1982.

Howell, Dr. Edward. *Enzyme Nutrition*. Wayne, NJ: Avery Publishing Group, 1985.

Humbart, Santillo. *Food Enzymes, The Missing Link to Radiant Health*. Prescott, AZ: Hohm Press, 1987.

Iyengar, B.K.S. *Light on Yoga*. New York: Schocken Books, Inc, 1976.

Kervran, Prof. C. Lauis. *Biological Transmutations*. Magalia, CA: Happiness Press, 1998.

Kravitz, Judith. *Breathe Deep, Laugh Loudly*. West Hartford, CT: INI Free Press, 1999.

Nelson, William C. "The Promorpheus" (visit www.qxsubspace.com for information).

Robbins, John. *Diet for a New America*. Walpole, NH: Stillpoint Publishing, 1987.

Schwartz, Gary E.R., and Linda G.S. Russek. *The Living Energy Universe*. Charlottesville, VA: Hampton Roads Publishing Company, Inc., 1999.

Szekeley, Edmond Bordeaux. *The Essene Gospel of Peace*. International Biogenic Society, 1981.

Talbot, Michael. *The Holographic Universe*. New York: Harper Collins Publishers, 1991.

Tompkins, Peter & Christopher Bird. *The Secret Life of Plants*. New York: Avon Books, 1973.

Vital, Mony. *Life Unlimited, An Exploration of Physical Immortality*. San Rafael, CA: American Pacific University, 1998.

Wigmore, Ann. *Be Your Own Doctor*. Wayne, NJ: Avery Publishing Group, 1982.

Wigmore, Ann. *The Hippocrates Diet*. Wayne, NJ: Avery Publishing Group, 1984.

Wolfe, David. *The Sunfood Diet Success System*. San Diego, CA: Maul Brothers Publishing, 2000.

Wolfe, David. *Eating for Beauty*. San Diego, CA: Maul Brothers Publishing, 2002.

Resources
and Suppliers

Blenders

Vita-Mix

8615 Usher Rd

Cleveland, OH 44138-2199

Telephone: (800) 848-2649

This high-speed blender will satisfy all your blending needs. It is expensive but well worth every penny. I would not be without it. You can start with a regular kitchen blender, but be aware that with the heavier recipes this type of common blender will not hold up.

Dehydrators

The Excalibur

P.O. Box 4133

Carlsbad, CA 92018

Phone: (760) 967-6664

Telephone: (888) 316-4611

This is the best dehydrator that I know of because it has a temperature control and all the trays are evenly ventilated and warmed. This dehydrator comes in small, medium, and large versions, according to the number of trays it contains. For a family I would recommend the large, for two people the medium, and for one person the small dehydrator.

Juicing Machines

Champion Juicer

Optimum Health Institute

6970 Central Ave.

Lemon Grove, CA 91945

Telephone: (619) 464-3346

Or

Rawfood.com

P.O. Box 900202

San Diego, CA 92190

(888) RAW-FOOD

The Green Power Juicer & the Green Life Juicer

7432 Fraser Park Drive

Burnaby, BC, Canada

V5J 5B9

Telephone: (800) 663-2212

(604) 435-4862

These juicers do it all. The Green Power is a larger and more expensive model, but they both do everything the Champion does and also juice wheatgrass. These two juicers are noted for maximizing the nutrient content in the juice.

Plastaket Manufacturing Company, Inc.

6220 East Hwy 12

Lodi, CA 95240

Telephone: (209) 369-2154

The Plastaket juicer can be purchased in many health food stores, although the Optimum Health Institute (OHI) and Rawfood.com have better prices. This is the manufacturer's address, which may have even lower prices. The same company listed here makes the Champion juicer, so price it through Plastaket as well.

Wheatgrass Juicer

Optimum Health Institute Store (try also Rawfood.com, address above)

6970 Central Ave.

Lemon Grove, CA 91945

Telephone: (619) 464-3346

OHI and Rawfood.com have a large, more commercial-type juicer for extracting wheatgrass juice, and they also sell a small kitchen model that works very well for one or two people.

Other Kitchen Gadgets

Citrus Juicer

Kitchen centers in any department store would carry this appliance.

Mandolin

This can be purchased at any kitchen center in a large department store.

Saladacco

See Optimum Health Institute and/or Raw-food.com.

Saladshooter

National Presto Industries, Inc.

3925 N. Hastings Way

Eau Claire, WI 54703-3703

Telephone: (800) 877 0441, (715) 839-2209

This electrical grater and slicer is very quick and efficient for grating or slicing vegetables, nuts, and seeds.

Seed Grinder (coffee grinder)

This is the same electrical appliance that is used to grind up coffee beans. It can be purchased at any kitchen center in a large department store.

Health Retreats

Ann Wigmore Institute

Ruta 115, Km 20

Barrio Guayabo

Aguada, Puerto Rico 00743

Mailing address:

P.O. Box 429

Rincon, PR 00677

Telephone: (787) 868-6307

Fax: (787) 868-2430

www.annwigmore.org

This health institute is similar to OHI and was started by the late Ann Wigmore, one of the founders of the Living Foods Lifestyle. It is situated one block from the beach and offers a warm healing environment to cleanse and detoxify the body. The diet is all raw foods, with lots of tropical fruits, vegetables, coconuts, sprouts, and living juices.

Hippocrates Health Institute

1443 Palmdale Court
West Palm Beach, FL 33411
Telephone: (561) 471-8876
Similar to Ann Wigmore's Institute in Puerto Rico and the Optimum Health Institute in California, this spa is geared for cleansing and detoxing the body, mind, and spirit. The diet of all raw foods is designed to clean the blood and bring the body back into balance.

Rawfood.com

P.O. Box 900202
San Diego, CA 92190
Telephone: (800) 205 2350, (619) 645-7282
www.rawfood.com
Rawfood.com has retreats in Hawaii, Arizona, and southern California. They specialize in fasting retreats, along with days spent hanging out with David Wolfe doing yoga and meditation, learning about the raw lifestyle, and enjoying sumptuous raw meals. This organization offers an abundance of amazing raw products and is at the cutting edge of sourcing the most nutritious raw foods from all over the world. Examples include their maca, cacao, goji berries, jungle peanuts, Hunza raisins, and much more.

Optimum Health Institute of Austin

265 Cedar Lane
Cedar Creek, TX 78612
Telephone: (512) 303-4817
Fax: (512) 303-1239

Optimum Health Institute of San Diego

6970 Central Ave.
Lemon Grove, CA 91945
Telephone: (619) 464-3346
www.optimumhealth.org.
This is a cleansing, detoxifying retreat center in the center of Lemon Grove, California, outside San Diego. It offers a relaxing and healing environment to cleanse and detoxify the mind, body, and spirit.

There is an open house at both Optimum Health Institutes every Sunday at 4:00 p.m.

Tree of Life Rejuvenation Center

P.O. Box 1080
Patagonia, AZ 85624
Telephone: (520) 394-2520
www.treeoflife.net
Gabriel Cousens, a leader in the living foods movement, founded this retreat center. It is a holistic live-food and integrative center that combines many programs to facilitate the rejuvenation of the body, mind, and spirit.

Culinary Schools for Raw Living

Living Light Culinary Arts Institute

Located in northern California

Telephone: (707) 523-9513

www.rawfoodchef.com

Taught by Cherie Soria, one of the top raw-food chefs, this institute provides a certification course in raw living foods for anyone interested.

Specialty Foods

Flora Inc.

P.O. Box 73

Lynden, WA 98264

Telephone: (800) 446-2110

Fax:(888) 354-8138

Flora sells a variety of organic cold-pressed oils, including flax, sunflower, sesame, olive, peanut, and safflower oils. They sell a combination oil called Udo's oil that is a blend of flax, sunflower, sesame, evening primrose, rice germ, and bran germ oils. It provides many of the essential fatty acids that we need to support our health.

Frontier Spices

2000 Frontier

Norway, IA 52318

Telephone: (800) 669-3275

www.frontiercoop.com

Frontier sells a variety of herbs and spices and different blends.

Gold Mine Natural Foods

7805 Arjons Drive

San Diego, CA 92126

Telephone: (858) 537-9830, (800) 475-3363

Fax: (858) 695-0811

Gold Mine supplies an abundance of Japanese products including a variety of organic, unpasteurized miso. They also have a selection of grains, beans, nuts, nut butters, and much more.

The Grain & Salt Society

273 Fairway Drive

Ashville, NC 28805

Telephone: (800) 867-7258

This company sells Celtic sea salt, which is one of the best salts to use because it contains many trace minerals. If you have high blood pressure it is wise to limit your sodium intake from salt. (Try also the Himalayan salt from Rawfood.com.)

Jaffe Bros. Natural Foods

P.O. Box 636

Valley Center, CA 92082-0636

Telephone: (760) 749-1133

Fax: (760) 749-1282

www.organicfruitsandnuts.com

Jaffe Bros. supplies a variety of organically grown, untreated dried fruits, nuts, dates, seeds, grains, and other select products for a health-conscious lifestyle.

Living Tree Community Foods

P.O. Box 10082

Berkeley, CA 94709

Telephone: (510) 526-7106, (800) 260-5534

Fax: (510) 526-9516

www.livingtreecommunity.com

This company sells many varieties of organic fruits, nuts, nut butters, and more.

Omega Nutrition Inc.
(Pumpkin Seed Butter)

Bellingham, Washington

Telephone: (800) 661-3529

www.omeganutrition.com

This company sells organic coconut oil, apple cider vinegar, flax and other oils, and the best pumpkin seed butter available.

Rawfood.com

P.O. Box 900202

San Diego, CA 92190

Telephone: (800) 205-2350, (619) 645-7282

For orders only: 888 RAW FOOD

www.rawfood.com

This company sells a variety of dried goods such as raw cacao, sea vegetables, and sun-dried tomatoes. They also sell books, dehydrators, flax seed grinders, juicers, and many other appliances that support a raw-food lifestyle.

Rhio's Raw Energy Hotline

P.O. Box 2040

Canal Street Station

New York, NY 10013

Telephone: (212) 343-1152

www.rawfoodinfo.com

Rhio offers raw/living food preparation classes monthly, as well as private consultations.

Rudell Enterprises

333 Orange Ave, #19

Coronado, CA 92118

Telephone: (619) 435-9066

In Mexico: (52) (624) 144-0769

www.Transform2000.com

email: wrudell@yahoo.com

Wendy Rudell, the author of this book, offers private consultations and hands-on food preparation classes, for both private individuals and groups. She specializes in gourmet recipes and teaches the theory of raw-food preparation so that individuals can open up to their own creativity.

Wendy designs private retreats for individuals and groups and is presently building and developing a state-of-the-art center for transformation and longevity in Southern Baja, Mexico.

The Spice Hunter

P.O. Box 8110
San Luis Obispo, CA 93403-8110
Telephone: (800) 444-3061, Ext 7000
(805) 597-8992
Fax: (805) 544-3824
www.spicehunter.com
You can purchase organic herbs and spices here.

Sunorganic Farm

P.O. Box 2429
Valley Center, CA 92082
Telephone: (888) 269-9888
Fax: (760) 751-1141
www.sunorganic.com
This company sells all kinds of organic dried fruits, nuts, seeds, grains, herbs, spices, and more. Their catalog is worth ordering.

Wheatgrass Direct

P.O. Box 249
Ottsville, PA 18942
Telephone: (610) 346-6687
(877) 558-4233
www.wheatgrassdirect.com
This company will deliver fresh, certified organic wheatgrass and sprouts (sunflower greens, buckwheat, and many others) right to your door.

Index

277

About the Author

Wendy Rudell has spent the last thirty-five years living a very healthy lifestyle and pursuing her interest in all the healing arts. After working as head chef of the Jam Factory, a large vegetarian restaurant in British Columbia, Canada, and attaining a teaching degree in the late 1970s, she became a coordinator and instructor for a Pritikin program in Maui that focused on reducing the effects of degenerative diseases. From 1984 to 1990, she owned and operated a raw food product manufacturing and distributing company on the island of Kauai.

Wendy has been studying and teaching Hatha and Ashtanga yoga for the past thirty years. She has been working with the breath since the early 1970s and has been a Transformational Breath facilitator and trainer for many years. She is now doing her own version of breath work called Ascension Breath. Wendy is also a licensed massage therapist, colon therapist, nutritionist, living foods consultant and chef, and is now incorporating quantum healing via advanced biofeedback into her array of modalities.

At the Optimum Health Institute in San Diego, California, Wendy implemented a complete program of lifestyle changes to support optimum health. The intention was to teach guests how to live a raw-foods lifestyle when they returned home. This included teaching gourmet raw food cuisine theory and application; cleansing and detoxification; breath work; yoga; meditation; and nutrition. Wendy currently lives in Cabo San Lucas, Mexico, where she provides similar programs to individuals and groups.

Wendy has developed the concept of "Transform 2000," a process of awakening the mind, body, and spirit. She has purchased over one thousand acres of land in the Cabo area to develop into a health and wellness community. For more information, visit her website at www.Transform2000.com.

David "Avocado" Wolfe is one of the world's leading authorities on raw-food nutrition. He is the author of *Naked Chocolate, Eating for Beauty,* and *The Sunfood Diet Success System.* Since 1995, David Wolfe has given more than 1,000 health lectures and seminars in North America, South America, Europe, and the South Pacific. He hosts at least six health, fitness, and adventure retreats each year at various locations around the world. He is currently a professor of nutrition for Dr. Gabriel Cousens' master's degree program on live-food nutrition. For more information about David's work, visit his websites at www.rawfood.com, www.thebestdayever.com, www.davidwolfe.com, and www.ftpf.org.